What People
FROM NERVO

Diamonds are forever! The Diamond Speech Structure is simply the best framework to build a "Nailed it" presentation every time. Its magic is in its simplicity and rule of three. I have the page marked for instant retrieval.

Katherine Crewe, P.Eng ICD.D FCAE, Chair, TEC Canada

Essential reading for all leaders wanting to advance their careers. Clear and concise guide from successfully improving your presentation skills to getting your strategy communicated effectively.

David Jones, Vice President of Engineering, Matrox Video

I've had the pleasure of knowing Suzannah long before I ever took to the stage. And, in those early days of trying to navigate the complexity of this business that is professional speaking, Suzannah was there for me as well ... countless times. When the doubt crept in. When I wasn't sure about the content. When the talk wasn't flowing ... Suzannah was there. Now the insights, wisdom and experience that took place behind closed doors is within these pages. *From Nervous to Nailed It!* breaks down the truth behind what it takes to make it on the stages (and screens) of the world today. Read this book and nail your next presentation!

Mitch Joel, author of *Six Pixels of Separation*
and *CTRL ALT Delete*

If you want to know about how to captivate and engage an audience while you deliver a speech, this is the book for you. Being a good speaker is a skill that will make you well known in your field and will open some doors for you as well. Not everyone is a natural speaker, but there are ways to ensure you can deliver a well-structured and engaging speech that guarantees to get your message across. And lucky for you, you will find these methods in *From Nervous to Nailed It!*

David Morales, FM Global Latin America,
Vice-President Operations Engineering Manager

From Nervous to Nailed It! is a masterful handbook on how to educate, inspire and persuade any audience every time you speak. Learning how to switch *from* being focused on what we, as speakers, want to say *to* what the audience needs to hear is the magic sauce that will transform any speaker's ability to have real and lasting impact. I will buy multiple copies of this book for the content of Chapter 3 alone. Filled with hot tips, ridiculous myth busting, super speaker stories and many other delights, this book will be an essential guide for all speakers and coaches.

Teri Kingston, TEDx speaker and coach
Founder, Real Impact Speaking

From Nervous to Nailed It! is THE Speaking Bible for every Entrepreneur, every CEO, every sales and marketing executive, and every not-for-profit organization looking to share their message and create a bigger impact. Suzannah not only lays out what to do to structure your speech, but also breaks down exactly *how* to do it. She includes topics like overcoming speaking jitters, how to have more fun and enjoyment, add more meaning – and also warns of those common pitfalls that can keep well-meaning speakers going in circles and feeling frustrated (and how to overcome them). Read this book and follow it step by step to dramatically change your speaking experience and increase your confidence.

Sarena Miller, Founder, Academy for Business Betterment

Whether you're a novice or a seasoned speaker, this book, filled with practical, inspiring, and insightful content, is a must-read! Suzannah's Diamond Speech Structure is nothing short of a gem; the synthesis of years of experience in preparing and delivering compelling content to her audiences and keeping them on the edge of their seat. If you want to add a scintillating spark to your message and nail it every time you speak in front of an audience, without any question, this book is for you. Simply brilliant!

Nabil Doss, Expert in Influential Communication and Speaker
2017-2018 President of the Global Speakers Federation
2013 President of the Canadian Association of Professional Speakers

This book is your fast track to developing the elusive "powerful presence" that every leader seeks to cultivate. Whether you need to make a clear and impactful point during meetings or you are called upon to step up to the mic at a major event, *From Nervous to Nailed It!* is without a doubt, your number one resource for success.

Corry Robertson, PCC Leadership Coach
and Director of Coaching Education

Just by starting to read the table of contents you will see that this is your one-stop shop, and a speaker guide to expand and fill your tool kit! This book is packed with value and is the roadmap you need to set up yourself for success. I appreciate how Suzannah covered everything, from how to overcome speaking mistakes, control nerves, and even tips about your stage shoes. With checklists, visuals, example stories and quotes, I can't wait to pull out my highlighter because I will read this book again!

Patricia Regier, MEd, Virtual Facilitation Specialist, Author,
Speaker, and Principal Consultant, Regier Educational Services

Every professional knows that finding their voice and presenting with confidence in any business field is essential. Finally, we have a real-world guide to unleash our speaking potential in this book. World-class speaking coach Suzannah Baum creates easily followed steps to achieve great success, speak with confidence, and impact the audience.

Gwen Mdinaradze, President & CEO, Speakers Alliance Canada

The principles of Suzannah's system are universal, and will help anyone not only understand how to communicate their message better, but will help them understand themselves better as well. Whether you are truly uncomfortable in any speaking or communication situation, or you are a seasoned pro, I believe that Suzannah's model will elevate your message. You will be able to get your message across more effectively, more naturally, and with less focus on your nerves.

Paul Frazer, PhD, Expert in Motivation Measurement,
Author, Speaker

Caitlin,

Wishing you the highest
levels of confidence,
clarity & connection in
all of your communications!

Suzannah Baum

SUZANNAH BAUM

FROM
NERVOUS
TO
NAILED
IT!

FIND Your Voice,
PRESENT With Impact &
UNLEASH Your Ultimate
Speaking Potential

For corporate inquiries and bulk orders please contact:
info@suzannahbaum.com

ISBN 978-1-7782229-0-0 (Paperback)
ISBN 978-1-7782229-1-7 (e-Book)
ISBN 978-1-7782229-2-4 (Audio Book)

First Printing

Editor: Catherine Leek of Green Onion Publishing
Cover and Interior Design and Layout: Kim Monteforte Book Design & Self-Publishing Services

To the shy, quiet ones who aspire
to share their message with the world.

To the bolder ones who speak up, stand out, and
strive to have an impact on those around them.

And to my mother, Lena, who lives
on in all I do every day.

CONTENTS

THE PROCESS WILL SET YOU FREE

Picture this …

You step in front of the audience with confidence. All eyes are on you.

Your strong opening immediately draws them in. You help them understand right from the start why this speech is relevant to them, and the value they'll gain from your presentation. Your entertaining, informative, and clearly structured content keeps them hanging on your every word.

The way that you frame the subject matter encourages them to consider a whole new perspective that will change their lives for the better. Your well-told stories entertain, inspire, and create connection. Your undeniable passion is contagious. The call-to-action persuades them to do what it is you want them to do, and your impactful close creates a vision of what the future holds for them. The end of the speech brings energetic applause, accompanied by appreciation and recognition for sharing a meaningful message.

You receive more requests to speak, and more interest in your products, services, and expertise than ever before.

The best part? Months after your speech, you bump into someone who was in your audience who tells you that as a consequence of your message, they made changes in their life – or business – that have produced exceptional results.

There's no doubt about it. You rocked it!

Don't you wish it was that easy?

Captivating vs. Just Plain Boring

When you're listening to a presentation, don't you love being captivated by the speaker and knowing that they have worked hard to make their presentation interesting, valuable, and relevant to you? The kind of speaker who has you glued to your seat as they deliver extraordinary value? The kind of speaker who makes you feel like they *know* you, even though you've never met?

On the other hand, isn't it a huge bummer when you're in the audience of an unengaging speaker – with no focus, no structure, and no clear point? Aren't you disappointed when you feel like the speaker couldn't be bothered to do even the bare amount of research to make the presentation relevant to you? And now you've given up precious time from your life that you can never get back.

So, which speaker are you?

Of course, you *want* to be that captivating speaker. You want to engage your audience, inspire them to action, and deliver value. You also want to build your visibility, enhance your reputation, share your expertise, inspire others, move projects forward, land that meeting, make the sale, gain trust, know that you're making an impact, and – yes, I'll say it – get some recognition and a whole load of compliments afterwards.

But what if you're *not* born with the innate talents of that captivating speaker? And if you're not, how can you recognize that fact, and turn it around quickly? How do you figure out what it takes to really nail your presentation?

Since you've picked up *From Nervous to Nailed It!*, it's fair to say that you understand that public speaking is one of the *best* ways to become known as an expert in your field, mobilize and inspire your team, create confidence and loyalty among your customers or followers, and grow your brand, business, or career.

There are many speakers out there who have deep experience and tons of brilliance. But all the experience and brilliance in the world is meaningless if you can't get your point across in the way that the audience needs to hear it. Your message will get lost if the structure isn't clear, if you're not framing the content the right way, if the audience isn't following along, and if the value isn't obvious.

With that said, how can you ensure that you're delivering structured, engaging, and powerful presentations, and that you're captivating your audiences each time you step up in front of them? What do you need to do in order to make your message clear and engage your audiences?

In short, what do you need to do to truly unleash your ultimate speaking potential?

We're going to work through that process together in this book.

Where Do *You* Fit In?

Maybe you're new to speaking and need help because:

1. You're afraid of public speaking;
2. You don't have the time to craft the perfect speech;
3. You don't know what to say or where to begin to create a compelling presentation.

Maybe you're already a fairly experienced speaker who works hard and spends huge amounts of time putting together presentations, but you don't get the follow-up, or other results that you expect after you speak.

Maybe you're a seasoned speaker, who gives good presentations that earn you decent feedback – but you instinctively know that you can be better, and you're ready to do what it takes to get better, engage and connect with your audience more deeply, and be outstanding.

WHO IS THIS BOOK FOR?

This book is for those who want to improve their speaking skills at work – the CEO or high-level executive who needs to communicate strategy, inspire with a meaningful message, and persuade the team towards action; the project manager who needs to pitch the team's ideas to the board; the brilliant doctor who is regularly called upon to give lectures to students but has trouble placing all the crucial elements into a concise, focused format that is easy for the audience to digest.

It's also for those who are feeling called to advocate for change – the leaders or volunteers of an association or non-profit organization who want to motivate, inspire, or persuade an audience to see through different eyes, take action, or make – or reconsider – a decision.

Basically, *From Nervous to Nailed It!* is for the experts, entrepreneurs, professionals, academics, and visionaries who want to get more deeply involved in public speaking to share their expertise, enhance their speaking skills, impact an audience, build trust, get visibility, sell services and products, and be recognized as leaders in their field.

In other words, if you do *any* kind of public speaking and would like to expand your skills, this book is for you. We'll work on getting you comfortable, prepared, and excited about creating speeches that grab your audience by their ears and hearts. You will discover a unique process and a multitude of strategies to make it easier and faster for you to build killer presentations that share focused and relevant messages, engage your audience, and get you the results that you want, each and every time you speak – whether it's to an audience of one, one hundred, or one thousand.

The Signature System

"How can I make my presentations better?"

"How can I get my audience to care about what I'm saying as much as I do?"

These are two questions I get asked all the time.

While it may be difficult to give you a thorough analysis of what constitutes a great speech in the first chapter, hang tight, because that's actually what the rest of this book is about. However, I can offer you the short answer in three words.

Confidence. Connection. Structure.

Without *confidence* to deliver your message and self-assurance in the strength of your message, you may end up hiding in the background, grudgingly giving presentations that are just "good enough," rushing through them to "get it over with," or declining opportunities to speak altogether.

Without an authentic *connection* to the audience, it's difficult for them to engage with you, or trust that what you're saying will make a difference to them.

Without a well-defined speech *structure*, it's hard for your audience to follow your message, and for you to stay on track with your content.

So, while structure is crucial to presenting a focused message, connecting to your audience is what will pull them in to take the journey with you. And confidence is what will compel you to get up in front of them and deliver a valuable message.

When I give this answer, people nod their heads and agree.

But then without fail, they follow up with, "But *how?*"

And that, my friends, is an excellent question.

"But *how?*" is the journey I invite you to take with me in the following chapters of *From Nervous to Nailed It!* It's what I teach in my corporate training programs, my keynote presentations, online courses, and with every executive speech coaching client I have.

"But, *how?*" is the key component that separates a "good enough" presentation from one that truly captivates the audience, delivers value, and leaves them wanting more.

In this book, I'll share the "But *how?*" through case studies, examples from speakers at all levels, and reveal all aspects of my Signature System.

Whatever your reason or motivation for public speaking, by the time you're finished reading this book, you will have a powerful set of tools that can be applied to every speech, presentation, or pitch you give. You'll be able to use my Signature System to craft a structured, engaging, and truly compelling speech that:

- you'll feel confident giving anywhere;
- you're proud of and that delivers value to your audience;
- captivates, shares your message, demonstrates your unique expertise, and inspires your audience to take action; and
- showcases *you* as a trusted and respected leader.

My Promise to You

Within these pages, we'll go from overcoming nerves to pinpointing exactly what is relevant to the audience, to narrowing your content down to a focused message, and creating a structure that is easy for both you and your audience to follow, to understanding the myths that hold us back from more effective audience connection, to using stories for better engagement, to gaining control of your delivery techniques, and so much more.

From Nervous to Nailed It! will not only help you deliver value, but also exceed audience expectations, mesmerize the crowd, position you as an expert and a leader, and have them lining up to learn more from you.

And then you can enjoy the rewards, recognition, and results that come with truly unleashing your ultimate speaking potential.

CHAPTER 1

The Problems with Presentations: And How to Fix Them

"YOU NEED TO KNOW HOW TO GIVE
A GOOD TALK IN PUBLIC. BECAUSE
SO FEW PEOPLE WANT TO TALK IN
PUBLIC SO YOU WILL STAND OUT."

James Altucher

The Day You Were *Almost* a Speaking Superstar

Imagine that after belonging to a business professionals association for several years, you've recently volunteered to join the Board of your local chapter to help grow and manage it. You soon discover that your branch doesn't have enough new members, retention is decreasing, and members are not as engaged as they could be. Special projects aren't moving forward, volunteers aren't volunteering, and fewer members are coming out to events.

You know it's a problem, your members know it's a problem, and national headquarters is starting to apply pressure, advising that if these problems persist, they may have no choice but to shut down your chapter.

Of course, the Board doesn't want that to happen and dives into figuring out how to fix these problems. They come up with a new vision, a new, fresh, and spectacular plan for the next year that will increase membership, drive volunteer engagement, and create more member benefits.

All that's left is for someone from the Board to present this brilliant new vision when the members gather at the annual general meeting.

And that someone is you.

But that's fine because, as a business professional, you give presentations all the time. You present to senior management, clients, your team, and all manner of stakeholders. You communicate, coordinate, negotiate, stimulate, captivate, activate, and maybe, if all goes well, celebrate.

So, this presentation – communicating the bold new vision for your chapter – is in very good hands.

The first thing you do is put aside some time to actually *think* about what you want to say. You start with some initial talking points. You choose your words carefully, and make sure your key messages are there.

You proudly share your work with the Board and they say, "Great! Go for it!" You can't help but think that they're delighted that *you* volunteered to take the lead on this presentation, and that now they're off the hook.

You've given up sleep to get this done, you passed on some personal commitments, and your family and friends can't understand why you're putting so much time into a volunteer position. But you know that this is a big opportunity. Many of the members are successful business owners and executives, and you want to make a good impression on this elite group of people. After all, this association has helped you expand your network and grow your business, and you never know when you'll need the help of these members in the future.

On top of that, the future of your chapter is on the line.

You know that you've got to be crystal clear about what *you want to say* in this presentation. You really need to drive those results home – to increase membership, propel volunteer engagements, and create more member benefits.

Presentation day finally comes. And how does it go?

Amazing!

Your buddy on the Board, together with one of the senior members of the chapter and a director from National, come up to you afterwards to pat you on the back and tell you what a great job you did. "The chapter is in good hands," they say.

You totally nailed it!

But then?

Nothing happens.

Week after week. Month after month. Nothing changes.

With every prospective member who doesn't join, with every volunteer committee that doesn't get the job done, with every new member benefit that doesn't get implemented, you are reminded that your presentation – the one that you worked so hard on, the one that everybody loved, the one that was supposed to change everything – simply did not get the results you wanted.

If you recall, back in the opening, The Process Will Set You Free, we compared the types of speakers we love – the captivating ones – and the kind we don't like to listen to – the boring ones.

The boring speakers are not even an option for us, so there's no sense in discussing it. Right?

The captivating speakers are what we aspire to be. They connect with their audiences. They deliver value by wrapping their expertise into a focused and relevant message, and creating a connection helps them achieve the results they want.

Welcome to the real world, where our presentations are expected to get results.

Dare to Step Up

 If you're a working professional, it's almost guaranteed that at one point in your career, you'll have to speak in public. Fortunately, there are many tools to make this process easier.

If you're a working professional, it's almost guaranteed that at one point in your career, you'll have to speak in front of others. Whether a networking infomercial, a make-or-break sales presentation, speaking up at a meeting, presenting a project update, delivering strategic reports, or taking to the mighty stage, you want to take your speaking opportunities to the highest level so that you stand out. You want to make it worth your time, energy, and effort by learning and applying public speaking tools that will turn your hard work into real results.

Some people may believe that it's easier to avoid giving the presentation altogether. Why put yourself through the stress – not to mention the added time, effort and hard work – that delivering a presentation requires, when there's so much else you can be doing with your life?

*But wait! Isn't it easier to just **not** give the presentation?*

You can always say no. Or ask someone else to give it in your place. Or run away screaming.

But should you? *Hint:* If you're reading this book, I think you already know that the answer is a big, fat "NO!"

In the following example, the company made an exceptionally unempowering choice because the *rest* of the marketing team was too nervous to present, too stressed about having to do any public speaking, and begged their supervisors to let them out of it. So, while my client was taking initiative by working with a coach to enhance her speaking skills, her team spent their time lobbying their supervisors to skip it altogether. That way, they wouldn't have to deal with the nervousness, the rehearsals, or, you know, the actual *work* required to present in a way that engages an audience.

Nor would they receive any of the rewards, recognition, and results that could have come with it.

The company could have supported the marketing group by giving them opportunities to grow their visibility in front of the sales team, build their speaking skills, and push them to attain new – and challenging – goals. Achieving those objectives would have ultimately benefitted both the employee *and* the company in the future. Instead, the company just let them off the hook, and let them give up. Just like that.

But that's not what *you're* all about.

So, let's roll up our sleeves and look at the most important, valuable, and audience-centric tools that, when implemented and practiced consistently, will dramatically enhance your visibility, improve your presentation skills, deliver value to your audience, and help you achieve the speaking results you want.

One Step Forward – Then Pushed Back

I once coached a client on an important presentation that she had to deliver to her company's sales team where she, and other members of her marketing department, had to present the new product updates and marketing strategies for the next quarter.

Over five intensive sessions, we restructured her presentation, created engaging elements, shared relevant stories and examples, and rehearsed extensively. She worked at a toy company, so we used some of their products as props to make the presentation even more entertaining. We established a call-to-action to help her sales team understand their next steps, including suggestions of what they should say when in their client meetings, so that they could drive interest, engagement, and, ultimately, sales.

It was really shaping up to be a focused, strategic, and fun presentation.

Before our final session together, where we would wrap it all up with final content tweaks and additional rehearsal, she called me with some surprising news.

She told me that the company changed their presentation strategy completely. All the presenters in the marketing team – including her – were now going to present to the sales team via a pre-recorded voice-over that would run along with their slide deck. That way, the marketing team wouldn't have to present in person, in front of the actual sales audience.

In other words, because most of the sales team were not comfortable with public speaking, the company decided that they would not have to deliver any live, in-person presentations anymore. Ever.

I'm sorry … they did WHAT?

It Takes Work, But the Rewards Are Worth It

Giving a successful presentation takes work. You have to think about what you want to say, come up with new ideas, put it into a structure, create slides, practice, deliver it to your audience, manage your nerves, and hope that your message is received in the way you intended it.

Or, it can take no work at all. You could get up in front of the room, "wing it," and hope your audience appreciates your innate brilliance.

On top of all that, audiences have high expectations of speakers. They want to be educated, they want to be inspired, they want to be entertained, they want to understand *why* what you're saying is relevant to them. If people are going to make the effort to come to your meeting and listen to your presentation, it had better be good!

We definitely all have enough obligations pulling at our time, so sometimes it's just easier to plug away behind a computer or in front of one-on-one clients than spend time working to create an outstanding presentation *and* not faint from the terror of standing in front of a room full of people.

But here's the kicker. If it wasn't for the fact that speaking is *the number one way* to gain credibility as an expert in your field, step up your reputation and visibility, and drive your career or business, you probably wouldn't have picked up this book.

 Speaking is *the number one way* to gain credibility as an expert in your field, step up your reputation and visibility, and drive your career or business.

Public speaking takes work – but if you put in the effort, the rewards are immeasurable.

And now that you have, there are no longer any reasons to avoid a business, personal, or career opportunity because it requires you to speak in public.

Tuning in to the Expertise, Knowledge, and Value That You Already Have

Several years ago, I attended a conference dedicated to women's growth, empowerment, and enlightenment. I was fortunate to meet a number of amazing and inspiring women, each one with a vastly different perspective when it came to public speaking.

I met the owner of a hugely successful business with over 50 employees, who said that she would be interested in doing more public speaking, but didn't feel like she had anything worthwhile to share with an audience.

I met a naturopath who had traveled the world studying her craft and building her knowledge to a level that most people are never able to attain, but wasn't comfortable sharing with an audience what she learned about different health and healing techniques among different cultures.

I met a financial advisor who preferred working one-on-one, and not sharing her vast knowledge and experience with larger groups because it was just easier not to.

What I strongly felt that these women needed – and don't get me wrong, this happens with men too – was a gentle prodding to help light a fire within them, to remind them that their expertise and experience *is* worth sharing, their stories *are* interesting enough, and that they *do* have extensive knowledge that is both valuable and important to share with larger groups.

Were they looking for permission? Support? A kick in the butt?

Maybe, probably, and yes.

Once they realized that people *wanted* to hear what they knew, there was no stopping them.

And once you realize that people want to hear what *you* know, there will be no stopping you either.

It's cool, fun, and rewarding when you realize that people want to learn what you have to teach. But more importantly than that, we have a duty to share our knowledge, experience, and talents, not just for our own professional gains, but because this information can help change the lives of people who are listening to us.

Which Type of Speaker Are You?

Typically, most individuals fit into one of three categories of speakers.

1. The Emerging (or Nervous) Speaker
2. The "Get 'Er Done" Speaker
3. The High-Profile Seasoned Speaker

Each type has varying levels of both skill and difficulty in public speaking. Where would you identify yourself?

#1 – THE EMERGING (OR NERVOUS) SPEAKER

The Emerging (or Nervous) Speaker has a hard time dealing with nervousness, as well as feeling overwhelmed with how to put a presentation together. They may be new to speaking in public. They may avoid it whenever they can. They make up excuses, suggest other colleagues present in their place, or just plain refuse when asked to give a presentation. They don't know what to say or where to start in creating a compelling presentation. If they have no choice but to give a presentation, they'll want to get it over with as quickly as possible.

The Emerging (or Nervous) Speakers tend to say:

- "I'm really not comfortable with public speaking."
- "Public speaking is not for me."
- "I'm fine speaking to one or two people, but when it's a group – I'm terrible!"
- "Can you give the presentation for me?"
- "Fine, I'll do it. Let's just get it over with."
- "Sometimes I freeze up, and all I can think about is how nervous I am – and I'm sure that the audience can tell."

#2 – THE "GET 'ER DONE" SPEAKER

Typically, this is a more experienced speaker who spends a fair amount of time putting together presentations and workshops. Nerves or no nerves, it doesn't matter, they just get it done. They may be consultants, leaders, corporate executives, non-profit representatives, or salespeople who would *like* to engage their audience, sell their products, book more meetings, and get good results, but their primary goal is to get the speech done – and then move on to the next priority.

The "Get 'Er Done" Speakers tend to say:

- "My presentations are good enough to get the job done."
- "Giving presentations is part of my job, so I just do it."
- "I've got six presentations next week, so I've got to pump out the slides fast."
- "Sometimes I get nervous when giving presentations or speeches, but once I get going, everything is OK."

#3 – THE HIGH-PROFILE SEASONED SPEAKER

This kind of experienced speaker has to give presentations often as part of their job, sometimes with very short notice. Recognized as leaders and authorities, they know that people look up to them, so they feel a responsibility to communicate with impact so that they can continue inspiring others as a role model. Already skilled at presenting, they tend to be more concerned with speech structure and focus, crafting a compelling message, and ensuring that their audience is engaged and ready to take action. These types of speakers strive to continually improve their speaking skills, because they know that they can *be* better but they aren't sure what steps they need to take to get to that next speaking level.

The High-Profile Seasoned Speakers tend to say:

- "I give presentations all the time, and I'm good – but I know that I can be better."
- "I give the presentation, everyone *seems* on board with the next steps, but then things don't change as I had hoped they would."
- "I need to get better results from my presentations."
- "I want to be seen as a trusted leader."
- "I want to connect with my audience, get them engaged, and make them *want* to take action – and not just take action because I tell them to."

THE DIFFERENCE YOU CAN MAKE

 Debating whether or not you should say "yes" to giving a presentation? Instead, ask yourself, "How would it feel to know that my message has made a difference in my audience's professional or personal lives?"

Whether you're feeling confident or nervous, whether you want to give the presentation or want to run away, or whether you're looking for greater visibility or want to dive into the nearest cave, ask yourself this question: "How would it feel to know that my message has reached my audience and made a difference in their professional or personal lives?"

Would that impact your business relationships, your confidence and your success?

It sure would. A lot.

For all the presentations you may have to give – the proposals, the sales pitches, the updates to management or your team, the stories, the new project you want to spearhead – there are big benefits to you and your business if you want to knock it out of the park with powerful presentations.

While determining what type of speaker you are is important so that you know your starting point in this book, it absolutely does not mean that this is where you're destined to stay through the rest of your public speaking life.

The Top Six Public Speaking Mistakes Even the Experts Make

Before we start discussing all the things that you can do to build or improve your speaking skills, it's important to take a look at what to avoid so that you don't create any bad habits or, worse, spend your valuable time focusing on the wrong things. With that in mind, here are six of the most common public speaking mistakes that even the most seasoned speakers make.

Learn to recognize and avoid the most common public speaking mistakes, so that you don't create any bad habits, or spend time focusing on the wrong ideas.

1. OVERCONFIDENCE

Some speakers feel that confidence is the sole predictor of speaking success. In other words, if they don't suffer from speaking nerves or anxiety, they're obviously better public speakers than most, and therefore don't need any help, thank you very much. They are just as likely to feel that "winging it" or "speaking from the heart" (otherwise known as "not preparing in advance") is an appropriate way to face an audience.

Here's the truth. Public speaking confidence does *not* equate to public speaking excellence. Confidence may give you a slight advantage when you step in front of your audience, but if the content isn't strong, if it's not structured, focused, engaging, and relevant to the audience, and if it's not delivered with impact, then all the confidence in the world won't take you far enough.

Ultimately, your audience doesn't care if you're feeling confident or if you're feeling nervous. To them, it's actually irrelevant. What the audience cares about is getting *value* from your presentation, and making sure that the time they invest in it is worthwhile.

In Chapter 2, we'll dive in with the first phase of the Signature System – *confidence*. We'll be looking at how to build confidence and manage anxiety as it relates to public speaking. You'll learn ways to manage your speaking nerves and dispel some of the prevalent myths of public speaking. You'll also discover the one surprising thing that will make or break your presentation – which also offers a convenient "side effect" of helping you build your confidence!

2. THE INFORMATION DUMP

Speakers who practice "information dumping" present their knowledge and expertise, but not in a way that is meaningful – or often understandable – to the audience. They give all the right information – *all* of it – facts, details, statistics, numbers, theories, hypotheses, they quote other experts, and sometimes even add in the kitchen sink. They do not necessarily create an experience for the audience that fosters greater interest or understanding of the topic, or makes them want to learn more. They overload their audiences with so much content that they can't possibly remember everything. And whether it be from boredom or feeling overwhelmed by the information, the audience often doesn't *want* to remember it either.

When you can create a message that takes your audience's needs into consideration, when you can tailor your message for them in such a way that they truly get what you're trying to say, and when you've made the effort to truly understand them so that you can get the message across in a way that they need to hear it, that's true speaking success.

In Chapter 3, we'll discuss how to understand what your audience needs to hear before you even start crafting your message. This way, you can ensure that the content that you build will be meaningful and engaging to them, so that you have a much better chance at connecting with them, sharing your expertise in a meaningful way, making an impact, and getting the speaking results that you want. This is the second pillar of my Signature System.

3. UNFOCUSED, UNSTRUCTURED, AND UNABLE TO FOLLOW

Often, the first concerns that my clients identify as their public speaking issues are related to confidence and delivery. These concerns include how to be more confident, how to improve their voice, how to stand, how to move, and what to do with their arms. While these are important elements to consider when presenting, they cannot be addressed until we start with *what* you say – the strength and structure of the content – and *how* your audience receives the message.

If there is no structure to your presentation – meaning, if you go off on tangents, if you bombard your audience with too much information, and if there's no logical focus and flow of ideas – your audience will simply lose interest.

The fact is that until you get your structure right, your message won't be clear. If your message isn't clear, your audience won't follow. And if your audience doesn't follow, there's no value. And if there's no value, what's the point?

A solid structure will allow you and your audience to stay crystal clear on your message, which is beneficial for you, when you're creating and delivering it, as well as for your audience, when they're listening to it.

In Chapter 4, we'll be looking at structure – the third element of the Signature System. We'll discover how to create rock-solid structure for your presentations using a unique, step-by-step approach that will forever change how you craft and deliver your presentations.

4. STORIES – TOO LONG, TOO BORING, TOO UNRELATED

Stories add color and life to presentations, make them more entertaining to listen to, and can help you engage, connect with, and captivate your audience. But they can also be self-serving, unfocused, and create a disconnect with your listeners. Without a thorough understanding of your audience – an understanding of who they are, what their challenges are, and why they've come to hear you speak, your stories – and your speech – will fall short of having the impact that can really reach them. The best content, the best stories, the best experience means nothing if the audience doesn't relate to it.

In Chapter 5, we'll be looking at the key aspects of storytelling, including a simple and effective storytelling structure, how to tell stories about yourself without looking egocentric, and how to build stories that add interest, entertainment, and immense value to your presentation.

5. DISTRACTING BELLS AND WHISTLES

This book wouldn't be complete without talking about *how* you deliver the speech, and the tools that you use – like your slides, and even your body – to present it.

First – your slides. They can be a wonderful tool that can engage the audience and hammer home your message, or they can be a tool that bores the audience and distracts them from the real star of the show, which is supposed to be you! Remember that your audience can't read and listen at the same time. As soon as you put on a text-heavy slide, or one with lots of text and images floating around, their eyes go off you and onto the slides. You don't want to compete with yourself for the audience's attention. Slides are simply a visual aid, and have to be approached with great care so that you remain the primary focus.

Second – you! Perhaps you're worried that your voice isn't clear, you don't feel comfortable, you need to work on your body language and gestures, you want to get a better sense of how to move around a room, what to do with your arms, and get clearer on all the technicalities of purposeful body language. And rightly so, because all of this is important.

But do you want to know a little secret for giving effective presentations?

The success of your presentation doesn't depend on how you stand, how your voice carries, what you do with your arms, or what the butterflies in your stomach are doing. It starts with what you say – the strength of your *content* – and how the audience *receives* your message. Once those pieces are clear, then you're in a much better position to ensure that the content that you so lovingly created is delivered in a smooth, confident way.

In Chapter 6, we'll discuss the good and the bad of slides and speech delivery.

6. NOT PREPPED FOR SUCCESS

Your presentation is planned. You've prepared, rehearsed, you're wearing your "power clothes," and you're saying the silent prayer shared by speakers all over the world: "May my technology work as it's supposed to, may I remember all my important points as I did in my second-to-last rehearsal which was the best one yet, may the audience laugh at all the right moments, may people think I'm brilliant, may I get lots of business or visibility within my company from this – in short, may I be awesome in every way!"

Silent prayer aside, there are a few things that can seriously derail your speaking awesomeness. Technology, traffic, timing, shoes that are too tight, and other terrible things can wreak havoc on the unprepared speaker. That's why Chapter 7 will show you what you need to prepare for in order to be awesome on the day of your presentation.

And when you've gone through it all, read this entire book, taken the notes, and integrated them into your next presentation, you will be able to confidently step into the shoes of a true speaking superstar.

*"Your careers will be determined largely by how
well you speak, by how well you write, and by the
quality of your ideas … in that order."*

PATRICK HENRY WINSTON

Your Audience Awaits

Sure, it takes time to craft an impactful presentation and, of course, you're busy and have other things to do. It's not always a picnic to deal with the nerves and anxiety of speaking in front of a room full of people, or to put in the work required to prepare the content in a way that is truly meaningful for your audience.

You've got to structure your presentation so that it's interesting, engaging, and valuable. You've got to deliver it with confidence, authenticity, and style. And you've got to ensure that you connect with your audience every step of the way. So yes, there's some work involved. But when did anything worthwhile ever come easy? Besides, once you make the decision to go for it, that part isn't nearly as difficult as you might think.

In fact, there is probably an audience out there right now, waiting for you and your message. Let's make sure they don't wait too much longer.

CHAPTER 2

The Little Speaker Who Couldn't: Confidence

"THE HUMAN BRAIN STARTS WORKING
THE MOMENT YOU ARE BORN AND
NEVER STOPS UNTIL YOU STAND
UP TO SPEAK IN PUBLIC."

George Jessel

Imagine the scene.

> The CEO is explaining the new marketing strategy that the company I'm working for is about to adopt. There are 45 of us in the room. As the CEO speaks, people around me are nodding, agreeing, and saying "great strategy!" But all that is running through my head is, "Something about this seems 'off' to me! He doesn't seem to be considering a few key issues that might blindside our progress!"

That day, I didn't speak up. I didn't share my concerns. In fact, I didn't say anything at all.

"After all," I thought, "if the CEO is saying it, and everyone else is agreeing with it, maybe I'm the one who doesn't understand. I'm not going to speak up and look stupid."

The CEO wraps up. The room is strangely silent. Then from the back, way in the corner, an IT guy pipes up and says, "Sir, with all due respect, have you considered the following issues that might blindside our progress?" and he went on to express the *exact* same concerns I had kept to myself.

Silence … aaaaawkward silence.

"See?" I thought. "This was exactly why I didn't speak up! It looks like he's going to get nailed. Good thing I stayed quiet."

The CEO pauses, looks at the IT guy, squints his eyes and says, "You know what, we totally hadn't thought of that. We're going to have to make some changes. Let's grab lunch today to discuss it more – my treat. Oh, and by the way, thanks for speaking up *now*, before we moved forward."

So, the IT guy got a free lunch with the boss and high-fives from the staff, just for speaking up.

Ummmm … *What just happened?!?*

The Sad Reality of "If Only"

Have you ever experienced the feeling – and the regret – of "if only"?

"If only I had spoken up." "If only I had done things differently."

At that moment, I could only imagine what could have been if only *I* had been the one to speak up and become the hero of the story.

I let fear keep me silent, fear of making a mistake, looking stupid, being judged.

How many times do you hold yourself back from showing your true abilities, your expertise, your opinions with the world?

As we grow up into adults, start our careers, and build our experiences, we're supposed to leave those worries behind and take our place in the world, speak up, be bold, and be unapologetically awesome!

Right??

That was *not* the case for me.

THE RELUCTANT SPEAKER

Growing up, I was extremely shy and quiet and, in my opinion, overlooked and ignored.

In those times when I mustered the courage to try to join a conversation amidst a big group or family gathering, I often felt that my opinions didn't seem to matter. I would speak up and they would change the subject, or talk right over me, like they never even heard me.

As a kid, I accepted that this was just the way it was. And as I grew up, I started to believe that whatever I had to say just wasn't important.

So, I stayed shy and quiet … through family dinners and holidays, through school, through my first few jobs.

It wasn't until that day, when *my* ideas went out to lunch with the CEO and the IT guy, that I started to suspect that if I wanted a prosperous future, I needed to get comfortable speaking up.

As a result, I joined a public speaking group. I attended the first meeting, where I was so traumatized by having to stand up and introduce myself that when I walked out at the end, I didn't ever want to return.

But I soon realized that my ideas (and I) would continue to be overlooked if I didn't make a change. So, six months after I walked out of the public speaking group meeting, I went back, along with a commitment that I would stay for at least three months, and give it my all. A few weeks into my return, I gave my first speech (with many reminders to breathe written directly into my script). It was terrifying.

Then my second speech. Still terrifying.

Then, my third! A little less terrifying, and a little more rewarding. But only a little.

Next, the strangest thing happened.

People listened!

A few months later, the public speaking group received a request from a university alumni association. They wanted a few volunteers to speak at their monthly meeting on the subject of public speaking. Feeling a little bolder after these three speeches, I volunteered.

What would happen if you didn't let fear of speaking up hold you back?

Oh, so much!

I was so nervous that day as those alumni professionals walked in. They oozed success. They wore custom-tailored suits, their shoes were shiny, and they had fancy pens. I *love* fancy pens.

A few minutes into my speech, two successful women in the front row – complete with classy, tailored suits and shiny stilettos – did something that changed the course of my career, and my life.

They pulled out their fancy pens and *wrote down* what I said.

They actually took notes!

What just happened?!?

In that moment, I was transformed. Those women gave me a preview of what could be. Was it possible that maybe, just maybe, what I had to say had value – enough to be willingly written down – with a *fancy* pen?

Leaving the event that evening, I knew something *big* had just happened. For the first time, I had clarity about what I was supposed to be doing with my life. I can honestly say it was *that* evening that sparked my desire to leave behind a career I wasn't enjoying in the field of marketing and sales, and take my first steps into building a business in professional speaking.

Still Feeling Nervous? You're Not Alone!

I've since learned that I'm not the only one who grew up feeling shy, quiet, overlooked, and ignored. Like some of the clients I've worked with, who you'd never expect had also spent a good part of their lives feeling shy, quiet, overlooked and ignored, I realized that I was not alone. There was:

- The entrepreneur who owned one of the most profitable retail franchises in the city, who *wanted* to speak about how she grew her thriving business but thought that no one would be interested in the strategies she used.

- The quiet, soft-spoken artist who had a fascinating background story that served as inspiration for her cutting-edge art but didn't want to share it with others because she thought they would find it boring.

- The brilliant graduate students who enrolled in the public speaking classes I used to teach. PhDs in biochemical engineering, literature, anthropology, dentistry, MBAs, all of whom were either too shy or nervous to speak to a group, or who were overwhelmed and unsure of how to focus their knowledge into a structured presentation, and therefore avoided speaking altogether.

The fear of speaking up and making a mistake, looking stupid, or being judged can strike us all. Whether you're an entrepreneur, a business professional, an artist, a PhD, a student – *anyone* – this fear can stop you from sharing the knowledge, experience, and expertise you spent most of your life building.

 The fear of speaking up and making a mistake, looking stupid, or being judged can strike us all. Don't let those fears keep you from speaking up and sharing your experience and expertise.

Since the start of my speaking career, I have worked with a wide variety of individuals and organizations with varying levels of comfort and ability in public speaking, and one thing has become very clear.

Each and every person has the potential to change their lives – and the lives of those around them – if only they would push the fear aside, speak up, and share themselves.

Today, I carry around a fancy pen wherever I go to remind me of the moment when my life changed. The pen reminds me of how far I've come, of how overcoming the fear to speak up – one time, for just a few minutes – radically changed the course of my life.

You have valuable experience to share. You can make a decision right now to speak up, no matter how shy or nervous it may make you feel. The feelings of discomfort are short-lived. The rewards of speaking up can last you a lifetime.

The Science Behind Nervousness

According to a 2013 study from the National Institute of Mental Health, three out of four people fear public speaking.[1] It can range from slight nervousness to paralyzing fear and panic. Many people with a fear of public speaking avoid these situations altogether, or they suffer through them with shaking hands and a quavering voice.

Have you ever avoided speaking opportunities for these reasons? Please don't.

If you're the kind of person who wants to share your expertise, tell your story, and provide value to large groups of people, or you get frustrated watching other people get credit for ideas that you had first but were too nervous to convey, then staying quiet and avoiding presentations is simply not an option anymore.

The simple fact is that you have spent a lifetime building your knowledge, experience, and expertise. You have tremendous value to share – and stories to tell – and you no longer have to let nerves, anxiety, or shyness taint your presentation style and effectiveness.

IT'S NOT *ALL* IN YOUR HEAD

Rest assured that public speaking anxiety is real and by no means "in your head." What happens to our bodies and minds when in the uncomfortable position in front of an audience can throw anyone off their game and make it more difficult to share their knowledge, expertise, and well put-together presentation. To better understand how to manage speaking nerves, it is equally important to understand *why* we are reacting in this way, so that we can better manage *how* to deal with it.

Believe it or not, the physical and physiological reactions that we experience when speaking in public are linked directly with the fight-or-flight response that our ancient ancestors faced.

For our cave-dwelling relatives, the fight-or-flight response was a result of a standoff with, for example, a saber-toothed tiger. When humans were around this kind of danger, their bodies and minds would have to very quickly decide if they should fight (i.e., the threat) or take flight (i.e., run away).

The part of our brains that regulates this fight-or-flight response is called the limbic system. Although our evolved brains are intelligent, our limbic system sees saber-toothed tigers and other risks like dark alleys, loud noises, and even public speaking, as equally dangerous threats. Public speaking threatens your vulnerability, your social standing, how people see you, and how you feel about yourself. It makes you extremely self-conscious. You feel like everyone is judging you. You may feel that if you mess up a speech you'll be kicked out of your social group – or kicked out of the cave, and straight into the waiting claws of that hungry saber-toothed tiger.

When you enter into fight-or-flight mode, here's what happens from a physiological perspective. Your hypothalamus triggers your pituitary gland to secrete the hormone ACTH, making your adrenal glands shoot adrenaline into your blood system. Your neck and back tense up, your muscles contract, your legs and hands may shake. You sweat. Your blood pressure jumps. Your digestive system shuts down to slow the delivery of nutrients to muscles and vital organs. You get dry mouth and butterflies in your stomach. Your pupils dilate. Your Spidey sense tingles. Basically, your whole body becomes trigger-happy.[2]

It's as if we see an audience as a threatening predator and react as if we're under attack. That's not very conducive to giving a speech, is it?

So, even with 200,000 years of human evolution, your brain still can't tell the difference between standing face-to-face with a saber-toothed tiger or presenting in front of your colleagues, clients, or tipsy wedding guests.

And because our brain is telling us that we are under attack, we do whatever is necessary to protect ourselves. We build walls between ourselves and the source of danger – in this case, the audience – to repel the attack and blunt any danger. What do these walls look like? We focus on our slides. We look down. We stand behind a podium. We read our notes. We avoid eye contact. In the process, we disregard the people in front of us, as we retreat into our protective bubble and wish them into invisibility.

But the nerves are totally taking over me! Why is this happening? And what should I do?

OVERCOMING THE PHYSICAL WITH THE RATIONAL

If you don't address what's going on rationally, these very real physical symptoms clog your brain's ability to guide your rational thought and steady your body movements.

The good news is that your rational mind still has some power to help you through this. Once you engage your rational brain, you can recognize that you've gone into fight-or-flight mode and talk yourself down. This can be very helpful in shutting down those extreme physical reactions. Something as simple as repeating to yourself, "This presentation isn't about me, it's about delivering value to my audience," can remind and refocus you, and eventually help you regain control and feel less nervous.

 The physical and chemical reactions that we experience when public speaking are linked directly with the "fight-or-flight" response that our ancient ancestors faced. The good news is we can engage our rational mind to help us through it.

So, the first step is to recognize it when it's happening, and then focus on what you *can* control.

The rest of this chapter addresses how to manage and then move beyond the feelings of nervousness and fear that might hold you back from presenting, so that you can feel more comfortable – and more excited – about speaking up and sharing your message with your audiences.

Six Tips to Control Nerves and Improve Confidence

Let's start with these six tips to calm your nerves and increase your confidence, so that you can kick your rational brain into gear and create a valuable speaking experience for both you and your audience.

1. **Prepare:** You have to know your topic inside and out. Research it, become the expert. Then you have to know your audience inside and out – who are they, why are they there, what are they expecting to hear from you, and what is their pre-existing knowledge of your topic? Create your presentation with that audience in mind. Also, if you're the type of person who needs to write down every word of your presentation in advance, do it. If you're not, then don't (although an outline can never

hurt!). When my clients get nervous at the idea of forgetting their content, I often suggest creating a one-page outline with all the key messages, and then setting it down nearby in case they need to consult it. Some will choose to bring an entire script with them. Ultimately, prepare in whatever way you need to so you can avoid "winging it" and calm those butterflies on the day of your presentation.

2. **Practice:** How you *think* you present and what the audience *actually sees* are often two very different things. Run through your presentation as many times as you need to so you are completely comfortable with the material. Do it out loud, from start to finish – and time it. This is the only way that you can fully practice what you're saying, how you're saying it, and how long it will take you to say it. It's an important show of respect to your audience to finish your presentation on time.

3. **Have a Backup Plan:** Think about all the things that could possibly go wrong and be ready for them. That could mean have an extra copy of your presentation handy, bring extra batteries for your equipment, be ready to give your presentation without your slides in case the technology melts down. If you have to cut your presentation short because of last-minute timing changes, be prepared in advance by choosing which content could be cut without taking away too much from your message, yet still allowing for your call-to-action and an impactful finish. Have water nearby in case your mouth gets dry. And arrive early, which has the dual benefit of allowing you to set up well in advance, as well as having a chance to meet members of your audience.

4. **Record Yourself, Then Watch It:** Record yourself – both audio and video – then take the time to listen and watch. It's the only way to know what your audience will hear and see. Is it engaging? Is it focused? Could you be saying something more clearly? Are you speaking too fast, fidgeting with your rings or your pockets, or swaying from side to side? Are you slouching or standing up straight? Can you fit in stories or examples to make a point with more impact? Are you doing all you can

to deliver a compelling message, or are you just trying to get it over with? And if you go over time, listen carefully to help you decide which content should remain and which content can be cut out of the presentation. Take notes, and coach yourself to make it better.

5. **Breathe:** If you find yourself short of breath, just take a moment to compose yourself, take a breath, and continue your speech. No need to apologize for it, because that only calls attention to your nervousness.

6. **Shift Your Mindset:** Stop focusing on how *you* are feeling – the nerves, the anxiety, the worries – and turn your attention to what your *audience* needs. Ask yourself:
   - Who will be in the room?
   - Why is this message important for them to hear?
   - How can I make it more relevant and meaningful to them?

When you stop focusing on yourself and start focusing on your audience, not only will you be in a much better position to provide value to them, but you'll also have much less time to focus on – and worry about – the nerves that you're feeling.

> *"The best way to conquer stage fright is*
> *to know what you're talking about."*
> MICHAEL H. MESCON

AFTER ALL THAT ... STILL NERVOUS?

The truth is, you may do all these things prior to giving your presentation and still feel nervous before stepping out in front of your audience.
That's OK.
Give yourself permission to be nervous. Go easy on yourself.
And then give the speech anyway.

 Using all the tools to manage your public speaking nerves, but still feeling nervous? That's OK. Go easy on yourself. And then give the speech anyway.

Five Ridiculous Myths About Public Speaking

Just as important as it is to learn the strategies required to help manage your nerves before giving a presentation, it's also very important to address how *not* to waste your time with some of the most prevalent – and silliest – myths about public speaking. Adhering to any of the fables that follow is a surefire way to make the learning curve towards managing your nerves and building your speaking skills longer and more frustrating.

MYTH #1: "Public speaking doesn't make me nervous, so I don't need any help with my presentations."

If you have mastered your fear of speaking in public, then congratulations! You're one of the lucky ones, and you should take advantage of that by getting in front of audiences and sharing your expertise every chance you get. Many people struggle with public speaking, so you're ahead of the curve. But if you remember anything from this book, remember this: Public speaking confidence does *not* equate to public speaking excellence.

> *Public speaking confidence does **not** equate to public speaking excellence.*

Just because you're not afraid or don't get nervous in the face of public speaking doesn't mean that you're off the hook or that you shouldn't continually strive to improve at it. Public speaking confidence will take you far, but if the content isn't strong, and it's not delivered with impact, and the audience doesn't care about what you're saying, then confidence simply won't get you where you want to go.

Some of my most successful clients are those who know that they're good at public speaking, but they want to get *better*. They want to have more impact. They want to engage their audiences to a higher level. They want bigger rewards from it. They want to be in front of more people, share their expertise before more audiences, and make the most of that opportunity.

MYTH #2: "I don't want to look too rehearsed or robotic, so I'm just going to speak from the heart."

Please no!

To me, "speaking from the heart" is code for "I'm not going to prepare, I'm just going to go with the flow and hope that the right words come out."

Don't get me wrong. Sometimes depending on the context, or the ability of the speaker, that kind of speech can work out just fine.

But the majority of the time, speaking from the heart can lead to a speech with no clear focus, no smooth flow of ideas, and too much disconnected information. The ultimate consequence can be that the speaker gets so bogged down in their stream of consciousness that they forget where they were going in the speech and have to find their way back to the main message. It can turn into a huge mess. It's not a situation you want to get yourself into when you're standing in front of an important audience – and every audience is an important audience.

As a speaker, you must know where you're going in your speech, and exactly what message you're delivering to the audience. It's not about you and your heart, it's about what your audience needs to hear.

Don't get me wrong, I'm not saying that you shouldn't share the knowledge, expertise, and gifts that are in your heart. Speaking from the heart only works when you've taken the time to tap into the message in your heart, in advance, when you have time to prepare and think it through. Then, when you're in that important position in front of that important audience, you're focused, ready, and know exactly where you – and your heart – are going in the presentation.

You're serving and respecting your audience when you create a structured speech that is focused, compelling, and engaging. Without that structure, it won't be clear. If it's not clear, the audience won't follow. If the audience doesn't follow, there's no value.

And if there's no value … what's the point?

MYTH #3: "I really don't enjoy public speaking, and I don't think I'm any good at it. So, can we just agree that I'm just not meant to do it?"

Nope!

I wish I could be more empathetic on this, but the truth is that despite whatever anxiety you're feeling, you can still create and deliver a presentation with confidence, clarity, and impact.

Over the past several years, I've worked with some people who feel that they suffer from a debilitating, all-encompassing, all-consuming fear of public speaking. However, I fully believe that everyone has the "speaker spark" in them. So, when I work with someone who has this level of discomfort, I will still gently nudge them outside their comfort zone to give even a short, two-minute presentation. And what we often find is that the very act of standing up and doing it – seriously, just standing up and doing it – is a huge win for them.

Sometimes just committing to it and giving it a try is all you need to do to find out that, in fact, you *can* do it. It may not always be pleasant or fun, and you may not love it, but you can do it, and you can do it well. You just need some practice, some guidance, some focus … and some sustained courage.

So, it looks like you're not off the hook.

I still haven't met anyone who I think is not meant to do any public speaking, but I promise to continue the search.

(Please take a look at Josh's Super Speaker Story (a little further on in this chapter) if you need more proof as to why you need to leave this attitude behind.)

MYTH #4: "The audience doesn't care *what* you say, they only care about *how* you say it."

I don't agree.

Performing and "emoting" in front of your audience will not be interesting to them if your content is unfocused, unengaging, and irrelevant, or if you are delivering it in an inauthentic manner. Likewise, when exceptional content is delivered in a monotone voice, too slowly, or in a way that doesn't have any personality or enthusiasm, your audience will not be able to engage with it either.

A popular-at-the-time UCLA (University of California, Los Angeles) study in the 1970s conducted by Albert Mehrabian claimed that when people are speaking, approximately 7% of the message comes from the words, 36% of the message comes from your voice and *57% of the message* comes from your non-verbal communication.[3] While there may be value in the discussion of how important non-verbal communication is when giving a presentation, I don't agree that it surpasses actual structured, compelling, relevant content in importance. It's worth noting that this statistic has often been misinterpreted, because it's difficult to quantify the impact of tone of voice and body language on the effectiveness of communication. It is very subjective, and interpretations of it differ from person to person.

Irrelevant content, even when delivered with passion and enthusiasm, will annoy your audience.

In summary, great content delivered badly will annoy your audience.

Structured content that is focused on your audience's needs combined with an enthusiastic, authentic delivery style that shows the speaker is equally interested in the topic are both equally important.

So, disregard those percentages, and focus on creating and delivering a presentation that offers extreme value to your audience.

MYTH #5: "If I tell my audience that I'm nervous, they'll be more empathetic and understanding if I mess up."

I once worked with someone who wanted to start her presentation with, "I'm very nervous, I don't do public speaking often, so please bear with me." Of all the ways that you could start a presentation, this seemed to be *the most* uninteresting way to do it that I could imagine. It provided absolutely no value – and no enticement – to the audience.

As speakers, our job is to engage our audiences within the first 30-60 seconds of our talk, to make them see why what we're about to talk about is relevant and beneficial for them. To start a speech with an apology, or a request to "bear with me" is a recipe for a whole lot of "meh."

Why did she want to start this way? Yes, she was nervous. This was one of her first public speaking opportunities ever. But the other reason was because she once saw a speaker start a speech this way, and she thought that it was authentic and vulnerable. She thought it acted as a subtle reminder to her audience to be empathetic and patient. And she thought that if she messed up, then at least she had a ready-made excuse. As a new – and nervous – speaker, that type of speech opening really resonated with her.

Here's why this speech opening is not only the wrong way to go, but it will bring down the energy and sense of expectation of your audience.

1. Admitting to an audience right from the start that you "don't do public speaking often," just as you're about to start your speech, can be a bit of a red flag that the speaker is an amateur, and the presentation may reflect that. Most audiences will come to a speech assuming that the speaker is an expert on the topic and expecting to learn something. By providing yourself with a ready excuse in case things go wrong, you may create apprehension in your audience that the speech may not be as relevant as they expect. In general, an audience doesn't know how nervous you are, so there's really no reason you should tell them.

2. As mentioned a few times throughout this chapter, an audience actually doesn't care how a speaker is feeling. It's not really about you and how you feel. It's about the audience – how to engage them, share a meaningful and relevant message, and bring value to them, so they are confident that listening to the speaker is a worthwhile use of their time.

3. Hoping that the audience will be more empathetic simply because you asked them to may not actually make them more empathetic. It's possible that they would have been anyway, simply because they're interested in the topic or because they're already kind and decent people who are already prepared to listen and give you their full attention, without you having to expressly ask for it.

In the end, despite sharing the many reasons she might want to avoid announcing her nervousness, the client insisted that she would still start her presentation this way. And while I disagreed, as her coach, I also realized that there was a point at which we had to move on and focus on other aspects of her speech.

But as a general rule, I stand by my opinion that starting a presentation by telling an audience that you're nervous is not a powerful or impactful way to begin.

Is Fear Short-Changing Your Life's Goals?

Over the years, I have met brilliant people who had so much anxiety over public speaking that they chose not to apply for certain jobs, they refused to present at meetings or conferences, or they dropped out of classes at school because it required that they give presentations.

Essentially, they changed the course of their studies – or their lives – in order to avoid public speaking.

So, I'll give it to you straight…

Sooner or later, if you have aspirations of professional growth, increasing your visibility, and sharing your expertise on a wider scale, public speaking *will* rear its not-so-ugly – and, actually, sometimes-thrilling-and-surprisingly-rewarding – head, and will find its way into your life.

NAILED IT! Think that public speaking just isn't "your thing?" Think again! Keep trying and keep learning. You may find that you can be surprisingly good at it – and enjoy it too.

SUPER SPEAKER STORY *Josh's Dilemma*

When I first met Josh, he had just taken a job as a Technical Sales Engineer at a major construction company in Montreal. One of the main components of this new job was that at least three times a week Josh would have to accompany the

Account Manager to customers and prospects to explain the very technical side of the sales presentations.

Josh really wanted this job, so when they asked him in the interview how he felt about giving presentations, he put on a big smile and said, "No problem at all!"

In reality, however, Josh was terrified of public speaking. He completely hated the whole idea of it. In fact, while he was already very well educated – he had both a Bachelor's and a Master's Degree in engineering – Josh told me that his dream – his *dream* – had been to get a Master's of Business Administration (MBA) degree. But when he found out just how many presentations he would have to give as part of the MBA curriculum, he quickly dropped his dream and got a Master's degree in engineering instead. While it certainly can't be considered a failure to have an advanced degree in engineering, the unfortunate part is how quickly he turned his back on getting an MBA because it required him to do so much public speaking.

Unfortunate indeed, especially since, years later, he was offered an amazing job that depended on his ability – and willingness – to engage in public speaking multiple times, every single week.

By the time he called me, Josh was in a bit of a bind. He was resigned to the fact that all his time spent avoiding public speaking was at an end. He would have to put aside his fear and do it anyway.

And he would have to do it *well* – really, really well.

He was very apprehensive of how he would be able to get over his nerves, improve his speaking skills, and deliver effective presentations once he had to start meeting and speaking to clients. But he was dedicated to getting through this situation, dedicated enough to hire a public speaking coach (that would be *me!*) to help him build skills that didn't come naturally to him. Those same skills that he never even wanted to focus on developing until then.

We worked together for several sessions, looking at the content that he was presenting, practicing it, and slowly weaning him off the boring company "script." We re-worded certain segments so that it was easier and more natural for him to talk about them in a more conversational way. We looked at emphasizing which parts would be most relevant to the audience, and devised strategies to engage and interact with them.

We implemented more structure to his presentations. He told stories of how other clients had succeeded based on the company's products and services. We created a more urgent call-to-action – even within the typical confines of a more informational, technical presentation. And we worked on having him deliver his message more smoothly and confidently, without any distractions, fidgets, or weird body language.

After his first client presentation, we got together to review what happened. How did it go? How did he feel? Was he nervous? What did he do about it? What did he do right? Did anything go wrong? Did he get a lot of interaction? What questions did the clients ask? How did they react to the presentation? Did they laugh at his jokes? What was the best part? What was the worst part? What feedback did he receive, from both his colleagues and client?

For that first time, he said that he was "satisfied" with his performance. He was satisfied at how he performed, how the client reacted, and, above all, he believed that his employer was satisfied at the results. It was very important to him to be able to display good-enough speaking skills that they would feel happy they hired him, and that he was the right person for the job.

All of this was great news.

But after the work that we had done together, and after he assessed the results of this first live presentation in front of the client and his colleague – he knew that he could do even better.

Whatever went right … and whatever went wrong, he soon realized exactly how much of the presentation experience was in his control. He was relentless in figuring out how he could not only *feel* better about his presentation, but how he could make it a better experience for the audience, so that he could get better results for his company – and better recognition and rewards for himself.

We met a few more times. We assessed the results of his previous presentations and fixed the issues as we went along. After about four customer presentations, the craziest thing happened.

He liked it.

He came to our meetings with such excitement, eager to tell me about how he made the audience laugh, about a conversation with an audience member that turned into an engaging group discussion, or how his colleague thanked him for going above and beyond what was required to make the presentation a great experience for the client.

He talked about how much fun he had with his last audience, and how the client mentioned that he wished that most technical presentations were like his. He talked about the moment in the presentation where he managed to explain an issue that the audience had been experiencing and hadn't yet resolved, and that moment where they all "got it." He talked about how his boss pulled him aside to tell him that the client called his boss to tell him what a great experience it was to have Josh giving the presentation.

Great news, right?

Absolutely!

Fortunately, Josh's story had a happy, successful ending. His career veered into the public speaking direction, and he thrived.

And yet, what might have happened if, in the years before we met, Josh had spent less time avoiding public speaking, and instead spent more time saying "Yes!" to speaking opportunities earlier in his academic career? What if he had actually earned his MBA, and not given up that dream because it required him to give presentations?

Where would he have been if he realized years earlier that not only could he *like* public speaking, but that he could be *really good* at it?

We don't know. And we won't know. While Josh's story had a happy ending, the lesson here is that if you continue to tell yourself that you don't like public speaking, that it's not "your thing," and that you're not any good at it anyway … you'll never know if, in fact, you could learn to like it, if it could become "your thing," and that you can be surprisingly good at it.

With life experience, we evolve. Just because at one time in your life you avoided public speaking – for whatever reasons – doesn't mean that this is where you must remain in your life. In fact, right now, you may

If you continue to tell yourself that you don't like public speaking, that it's not "your thing," and that you're not any good at it, you may never know that you could, in fact, be a masterful speaker.

be ready for a new challenge, or to reach a new goal. You may be ready to share your expertise. And you may be ready to tolerate a little discomfort to get there.

If it's your time to shine, then it may just be time to let it happen.

While we've already covered Six Tips to Control Nerves and Improve Confidence earlier in this chapter, if you still find that the thought of giving a presentation or even speaking up at a meeting makes it feel like you've got butterflies in your stomach, your face is heating up like a burning stove, your palms are sweaty, and you're sure that everyone can see how nervous you are, there's one more thing that can help.

And it will make a *huge* difference every time you speak.

 A good speech structure makes it easier for your audience to follow your presentation, easier for you to present it, and easier for you to feel more confident.

Structure Your Way to Speaking Success

As you've probably seen so far in this book, there are many elements that need to come together to create a truly engaging, compelling presentation that's delivered in a smooth, confident way.

And yet, there is one element that stands out, that can absolutely make or break your presentation. This also happens to be the one element that will help you feel more confident, manage your nerves, and deliver a high-impact presentation that positions you as a leader.

Are you ready for it? Drum roll please!

It's all about – STRUCTURE.

Speech structure.

What, not exciting enough? Actually, it's incredibly exciting. Here's why.

- A strong speech structure will help you manage the fear, anxiety, and general nervousness of public speaking.

- A strong speech structure will show your audience that you put in the time to prepare the most relevant, meaningful speech content for them and their specific needs.

- A strong speech structure allows for greater clarity in the content, is easier for the audience to follow, and is easier for *you* as the speaker to present.

- A strong speech structure will allow you to share information that is valuable to the audience and build a strong connection with them so that you can better engage and influence them to take action.

When you build a speech that is strong in structure, targeted to the specific needs of the audience and shares a message with clarity and focus, your presentation becomes not just something that you give and hope for the best, but something that shares your expertise, knowledge, and talents while truly engaging your audience. You'll be delivering a meaningful message that connects with them, speaks their language and that provides value.

The excitement of delivering a powerful speech that has you, your personality, your expertise, and your unique value woven into it becomes much more powerful than the fear.

There's a whole lot more about how to build rock-solid structure into your presentations in Chapter 4.

Excited?!?

But wait ... there's more!

One Essential Step *Before* Building Your Speech Structure

Before we look at the magic of speech structure, we need to make a small detour. This is where we dive a little deeper into the process that allows you to better understand your audience and determine the right content for them, which will then be applied to create your rock-solid speech structure.

This "before-the-speech-structure" step is essential to ensure that your speech educates, inspires, and persuades your audience in a meaningful way, so that you can get the best results from it. With this essential step, your presentation will be the focused, relevant, and engaging message that your audience deserves.

Even more excited now??

Let's check it out!

CHAPTER 3

Your Path to a Killer Presentation: Connection

*"THE SUCCESS OF YOUR
PRESENTATION WILL BE JUDGED
NOT BY THE KNOWLEDGE YOU
SEND BUT BY WHAT THE
LISTENER RECEIVES."*

Lilly Walters

Structure is a critical part of any presentation – but you can't move forward in creating it until you have established a connection with your audience through meaningful and relevant content.

> **SUPER SPEAKER STORY**
>
> ### The Speaker Who Had It All – Except for His Audience's Attention
>
> Meet Pierre. Nice looking, quite tall at 6'4", he was the Chief Executive Officer (CEO) at a global insurance company with 50,000 employees and 120 international locations. Pierre was very friendly and personable, a great dresser, always wore stylish and well-polished shoes and was quite popular and well-liked among his employees. On top of that, Pierre loved public speaking in all forms

– which he had to do quite often with clients, prospects, employees, and management. He loved making jokes, loved being the center of attention, and made special efforts to take the formality out of his presentations in order to make his audiences comfortable.

Here's the problem he experienced that made him reach out to me. When he had to deliver corporate presentations – updates to management and employees regarding project plans, company goals, sales strategies, just about anything about the organization – he was *bored*.

Bored with the information that he was presenting and bored with how he was presenting it.

Not only was *he* bored, but he clearly sensed that his audience was bored too. So many technical details, so much strategic direction, data, information, statistics, and goal-setting content simply wasn't very interesting for him to present, or for his audience to listen to. As much as he tried to make the content more fun and engaging, he struggled with the fact that it didn't seem to be connecting with his audiences, regardless of how much energy he put into it.

When he had to present more corporate, "dry" content, his strategy was to give *all* the information to his audience, assign them their action items, and then expect them to run with it. In other words, he delivered the information from a *presenter-centric* perspective. He shared what *he* felt was important for the audience to know. Nothing more, nothing less.

Eventually, however, he started to notice that even though everyone nodded their heads and agreed with him when he presented this important information, and they committed to taking certain actions at the end of each meeting, they weren't following through. Action items were taking a lot longer to get done. Details were falling through the cracks.

Ultimately, he wasn't getting the results that he was hoping for.

He sensed that while they connected with him personally because they enjoyed his bold and fun speaking style, he would lose that connection once he shifted to presenting about more corporate matters.

He was left wondering why he was not getting results. And he was also frustrated because he was confident, and saw himself as a visionary, an influential leader, a motivator. He wanted so much to give presentations that matched his energy level, but he didn't know how to do that when speaking about "boring" corporate topics.

You probably already guessed that it had nothing to do with his topic. It had everything to do with presenting it in a way that was meaningful and relevant to the audience.

I first started by asking him, "*Why* would your audience want to do what you're directing them to do?"

His response?

"Because it's their job. And because it will help the company grow."

These responses were very focused on the company. In order to effect change, we needed him to start looking at them in a way that was more focused on the *audience*.

To build our more *audience-centric* message, we went back to the question, "*Why* would your audience want to do what you're directing them to do?" In other words, why should they care? Why is this beneficial to them? What value will *they* receive, separate from the value that the *company* would receive?

Did they want raises or bonuses for work well done? Promotions? Small tokens of gratitude, like a gift card to a restaurant, or a shout-out in the company newsletter? More strategic support, training, or coaching? Public recognition and appreciation? A simple "thank you?"

We really had to get clear on what the employees valued in terms of motivation and outcomes of their work. We also had to dig deep to further understand what kind of work they were doing, where their challenges were, and what motivated them.

When we started integrating this audience-centric approach into his presentations and discussing ways to present the content in a way that was more meaningful for the audience, it changed everything.

Not only did the audience respond in a much more positive way to what he was saying, but because the content was made additionally relevant to them, they were engaged to a greater extent and connected. As a result, there was now more space for Pierre to put his full personality into his presentation – but now, with far better results.

> With his energetic presence, his big personality, and more engaging, audience-centric content, not only did they reach their sales numbers, follow through on their commitments, and achieve their corporate goals, but he wasn't bored by his presentations anymore. And neither were his audiences.

Connection is possible in each and every presentation that you give. But sometimes, there are other factors at play that can make it a problem to attain it. Read on.

 Want to get better results from your presentations? Look at it from an *audience-centric* mindset; not a presenter-centric mindset.

The Problem with Most Presentations

There are many people who have deep experience, expertise, and knowledge, but their message gets lost because it isn't clear, they aren't framing it in a way that's relevant to the audience, and the value isn't obvious.

All the brilliance and speaking skills in the world are meaningless if you can't get your point across in the way that the audience needs to hear it.

So, how *does* your audience need to hear it?

And how is it that some people get it right, and others get it so very wrong?

Whether you're speaking to a group of one thousand people at a conference, ten people at a company meeting, or that one important person on the phone or sitting across from you, your presentations have to achieve one purpose – to get your point across in a way that is meaningful and valuable to your audience, so that you can get the results you want.

It can be harder than it looks.

Remember the scenario at the beginning of Chapter 1, where you worked so hard on a professional association presentation that took you hours to create, and then you delivered it to great applause and feedback, but then – nothing changed. There was no increase in membership, no change in volunteer engagement, and no creation of more membership benefits. What you wanted your audience to do ultimately didn't get done. In essence, you did not get the results you wanted.

The simple fact is that, far too often, time, energy, and resources are being invested in presentations that simply do not get the results that they were designed to achieve.

BRING MEANING AND RELEVANCE TO YOUR AUDIENCE

As presenters, we are taught that the secret to presentations that get results is to be crystal clear about what *we* want to say. However, while it is very important to be clear about what we want to say, if that's all we're focused on, then we won't get the results that we want.

And here's why. It's because we're focused on what *we* want to say, and not what *the audience* needs to hear.

Knowing this fact will help you avoid many of the common mistakes that speakers often make, such as:

1. Putting too much information into their presentation, resulting in a "data dump" that is too detailed, too overwhelming, and simply too much for an audience to take in.
2. Sharing information that the *presenter* thinks is important to talk about but has no relevance to an audience's current reality.
3. Designing fancy slides and sharing fun images and videos in your presentation in the hopes that the audience will enjoy watching them, but not relating them properly to the content.

When you focus on what the audience needs to hear, and then build your presentation from that perspective – only *then* can you build a connection with them, only *then* can you guarantee that the time, energy, and resources that you put into your presentation is well spent, and only *then* will you get the results you want.

> *"90% of how well the talk will go is determined before the speaker steps on the platform."*
> SOMERS WHITE

CREATE CONNECTION WITH A KILLER PRESENTATION

It's incredibly important to get clear on your essential message and how your audience needs to hear it well before you even start crafting your presentation. While this additional step may seem like something you don't need to address because "I already know what I want to talk about," it's critical to ensuring that you establish a connection with your audience by creating the right message for them.

If you do this part right, it's no longer just considered a well-structured speech. It is, what I like to call, a Killer Presentation.

What Exactly *Is* a Killer Presentation?

A Killer Presentation is *an audience-centric presentation that is crafted to educate, inspire, and persuade an audience so that you can get the results that you want.*

Let's break that down by defining each segment of that definition. For this particular definition, however, we need to start at the end – with the results.

Results

Frequently, speakers can get so involved in the mechanics of a presentation – the content, the slides, the delivery – that they end up putting much less thought into how they're going to achieve the actual end results that they're looking for.

 A Killer Presentation is an audience-centric presentation that is crafted to educate, inspire, and persuade an audience so that you can get the results that you want.

So, are you clear on exactly what *results* you are looking for from your presentations? What outcomes or goals do you want to achieve?

When I ask this question of my clients, very often responses may include:

- "To give a good presentation."

- "To make more sales."
- "To not feel as nervous as I do when I speak."
- "To get the client to the next level of decision-making."
- "To get my team, client, or prospect to take action."

These are valid starting points, but they aren't enough. Frequently, the results aren't determined in enough detail, and are considered an afterthought. The priority may turn towards creating a presentation that shares the necessary information, and that is delivered confidently – and then hoping that the audience "gets" it, so that the results are eventually achieved.

However, a slight shift in mindset can make all the difference in helping you define, and then achieve, the results that you want from your presentation.

> *"If you don't know what you want to achieve in your presentation your audience never will."*
> HARVEY DIAMOND

SHIFT YOUR MINDSET, SHIFT YOUR PRESENTATION

Although the concept of "results" comes at the end of the definition for a Killer Presentation, it's actually much more important for you to consider the results you want at the beginning, *before* you even start crafting your presentation.

Before you get up in front of a group or have an important conversation with a client, colleague, prospect, family member or friend, you need to get clear on the end results that you're hoping to achieve. Doing that will help you direct your presentation towards that specific outcome.

The results that you want to achieve can be both from a professional or personal perspective. For example, let's say that you have to give an important presentation to your workforce to motivate them towards adopting a new business strategy. The results that you're looking for can therefore include points like those listed below.

- Your team clearly understands the new strategy, and how it affects their day-to-day tasks (professional).

- They recognize, buy into, and are clear on what their next steps should be (professional).

- They understand why they're a valued part of the strategy (personal and professional).

- You feel that you've delivered your presentation with confidence (personal and professional).

- You position yourself – and are seen – as a leader (personal and professional).

The type of results that you want to achieve will vary with of your presentations, depending on the message, the type of audience, the reason for the presentation, the timing in the sales cycle, the number of people in the audience, the location, and a variety of other factors.

WHAT KIND OF RESULTS ARE YOU LOOKING FOR?

Take a look through the thorough (yet non-exhaustive) checklist on page 53 for some of the professional or personal results that you may want to achieve as a result of your presentation. The next time you have to give a presentation, pull out this checklist and consider which ones are most important to you – and to your audience.

Feel free to put checkmarks or highlights beside your desired results – and add some of your own!

Audience-Centric

An audience-centric presentation is one that is focused on what the audience needs to hear, instead of what the presenter wants to say.

As speakers, our challenge will always be how to present the information in a way that is meaningful and relevant to our audience. Anything less becomes the "data dump" that I mentioned before, which will bore, disengage, and frustrate your listeners.

Presentation

Merriam Webster defines "presentation" as *"an activity in which someone shows, describes, or explains something to a group of people."* Most of us

Checklist: What Speaking Results Are You Looking For?

Professional Results	Personal Results
☐ More money, sales, referrals	☐ The ability to share your expertise and knowledge
☐ New clients	☐ Be seen as a leader
☐ Bonus/commission	☐ Recognition and appreciation from your colleagues for your abilities
☐ Promotion	
☐ Brand awareness	☐ Professional development
☐ Social media likes, comments, subscribes	☐ More effective in job interviews
	☐ Enhanced confidence when communicating and presenting
☐ Enhanced professional reputation	
☐ Persuade investors	☐ The feeling of knowing that you "nailed" your presentation
☐ Respect and recognition from boss, superiors, clients, colleagues	☐ Ability to manage stress, anxiety, and nerves when preparing for a presentation
☐ Increased trust from your team, clients, and Board	☐ A reputation as a good presenter who delivers value
☐ Enhanced ability to motivate your team	☐ More confidence in saying "YES!" to your next presentation
☐ Your team is clear on their tasks	
☐ Public relations	☐ Requests to deliver more presentations because you'll be trusted to provide value
☐ Media coverage	
☐ Organization is seen as an industry leader	☐ New personal and professional opportunities
☐ Organization grows/becomes more profitable	
☐ Corporate awards or recognition	
_____	_____
_____	_____
_____	_____
_____	_____
_____	_____
_____	_____

tend to think of presentations as formal events, one person at the front of the room speaking and sharing information. But in today's world, presentations are so much more than that.

They include everything from two-minute conversations in the hallway, to hour-long virtual or conference calls to full-day Board meetings. They include that quick call with a prospective client, that interoffice communication, and that project update to your team.

Sometimes we're just presenting ideas to one person – our boss, our colleague, our client, our spouse, our child, our mother-in-law.

All of these meetings, conversations, phone calls, and communications are presentations, because the ultimate objective is not only to share information, but to achieve a specific outcome and get a specific result.

Educate, Inspire, Persuade

Earlier, we established how critical it is to create a connection with our audience. The ultimate purpose of this connection is to build trust, so that we can influence the behaviors we need, and ultimately get the results we want.

 Creating a connection builds trust between you and your audience. With this trust, you'll be able to influence the behaviors you need. With this influence, you are far more likely to get the results that you want.

The three objectives that will help us create that critical connection are to *educate, inspire,* and *persuade* our audiences – throughout our whole presentation. These three concepts are the foundation to building the most relevant and valuable content in every single presentation you deliver.

The three steps to creating that critical connection are to educate, inspire, and persuade.

Let's take a closer look at these three powerful words.

EDUCATE

The traditional definition of educate is *"to instruct or inform."* This is the part of the Killer Presentation where we want our audiences to *learn* something.

However, to educate an audience isn't just to instruct or inform them. It is to instruct or inform them in a meaningful way.

INSPIRE

The traditional definition of inspire is *"fill someone with the urge or ability to do or feel something."* This is the part of the Killer Presentation where we want to inspire our audiences to *feel* something.

So, if to educate is to instruct or inform in a meaningful way, to inspire is all about filling people with emotions, and triggering feelings. You want them to truly understand the value in a project, an idea or a task. You want them to understand *why* what you want them to do is important, *why* it is beneficial to them, and *why* they should desire this change and want to take action.

PERSUADE

The traditional definition of persuade is *"to influence someone to take action."* This is the part of the Killer Presentation, most commonly near the conclusion, where we want to persuade our audiences to *do* something.

If *to educate* is to instruct or inform in a meaningful way, and *to inspire* is to trigger feelings and fill people with emotions that give them the urge to act, then *to persuade* is about "closing the deal." It's about saying what needs to be said so that your audience knows what you want them to *do*, and increases the likelihood that they will follow through and do it.

In short, we want to persuade our audiences to take the steps, do the action, and create the change.

> *"Designing a presentation without an audience in mind is like writing a love letter and addressing it 'To Whom It May Concern.'"*
>
> KEN HAEMER

How Human Resources Slowed Down High Turnover – With Dental Insurance?

A company I once worked with was losing their top employees to the competition. Human Resources was asked to give a presentation about the organization's many benefits and perks to counter this situation.

At first, the presentation was all about the benefits offered by the company to entice the remaining employees to stay. The presentation focused on the health and dental insurance, vacation days, international offices, and career growth and opportunities. However, despite the fact that these presentations focused on absolutely everything that the company offered its employees, people continued to leave.

We sat down together to try to figure out why the employees didn't seem to care about these benefits. Why were they not compelling enough to persuade the employees to stay? Did they need to be communicated in a different way? And furthermore, what *would* make the employees care?

We asked ourselves, "What does the audience need to hear about the benefits and the company for them to *want* to stay?"

We realized that we had to educate the employees in a way that was meaningful to them. Instead of focusing on presenting the long list of benefits being offered by the company, we focused on how the employees could integrate these benefits into their lives in a way that would be valuable and useful for them.

With these updated presentations, Human Resources didn't just *tell* the employees of career advancement opportunities but provided them with real-world examples and shared interesting stories of employees – many of whom the audience knew personally – who had moved into different positions, and what their experience was like. This focus on sharing through stories helped the employees see the value of these advancement opportunities.

Human Resources didn't just *tell* the employees that they could work in international offices, but they laid out exactly how overseas employees were welcomed to these international offices, and some specific information about the country in which those offices were located. They included what the local food, lifestyle, and popular activities were like, and all the ways in which the company supported single and married employees, and their families in these international assignments. This allowed the employees to better visualize the professional opportunities, the cultural experience, and how they might realistically experience it on a day-to-day basis.

They didn't just *tell* the employees that the company offered health and dental insurance, but they shared stories of employees who benefited deeply because they had access to dental insurance when they – or their teenagers – needed extensive orthodontic work over a period of several years, travel insurance when their colleagues had troubles while on the road, and the value of getting regular physiotherapy or massages to help alleviate their aches and pains.

All of a sudden, employees weren't simply sitting back and passively listening to a huge list of reasons why the company felt that they should stay – but rather, they were creating a conversation, telling stories, and sharing a vision where the employees could see the full value of the benefits, as well as building more awareness about how the company cared about them and the many ways that they were both willing and able to offer them greater professional opportunities.

While previously, employees were leaving because they got a "better offer" at another organization – now employees were taking a much closer look at everything that the company offered them, the various levels of support available to them, and reconsidering their professional future as someone who could grow with the company, rather than leave it for something shiny and new.

Four months later, employee turnaround had decreased significantly, and the particular benefits that had been *meaningfully* identified in those presentations were exactly the ones that were being taken advantage of the most by the employees.

By educating in a way that was meaningful and relevant to their audiences, Human Resources was able to create a connection that built trust, so that they could influence the behaviors that they needed to get the results they wanted.

PUTTING IT ALL TOGETHER

Now let's take a step back and look at how it all works together.

We understand the importance of creating a connection with our audience. We know this connection will build trust between us and our audience. We acknowledge that this trust will allow us to influence our audience's behaviors. And we recognize that all these elements will bring us the results we want.

And as we have now learned, to create that critical connection, we must educate, inspire, and persuade our audience to reach a certain result. In other words, you want to:

- *Educate* your audience so that they *learn* what you want them to learn;

- *Inspire* your audience so that they *feel* what you want them to feel; and

- *Persuade* your audience so that they *do* what you want them to do.

In the next section, we'll explore the intersections in this Venn diagram and find the sweet spot where they all come together (see Figure 1).

Figure 1: Killer Presentation = Educate + Inspire + Persuade

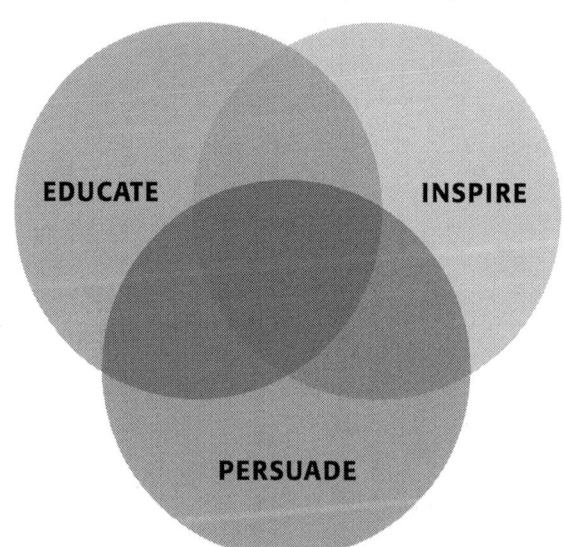

THE ONE WAY TO MAKE SURE IT'S *REALLY* A KILLER PRESENTATION

To ensure that the presentation that you craft truly qualifies as a Killer Presentation, you need to make sure that the essential components – that is, content that is designed to educate, inspire and persuade your audience – are in every presentation, every time you speak.

If we map these three essential components onto a diagram, we will find that the center point is the sweet spot of the Killer Presentation. Looking at the locations where two of these components meet provides us with questions – and answers – that will get us closer to this coveted sweet spot.

> *To truly qualify as a Killer Presentation, your content needs to educate, inspire, and persuade your audience.*

"WHY THIS?"

If you only inspire and persuade your audience, but don't devote enough attention to educating them on what you want them to learn, they may ultimately ask, *"Why this? Why is this important to me?"* (See Figure 2.)

Figure 2: Inspire + Persuade – Educate = Why This?

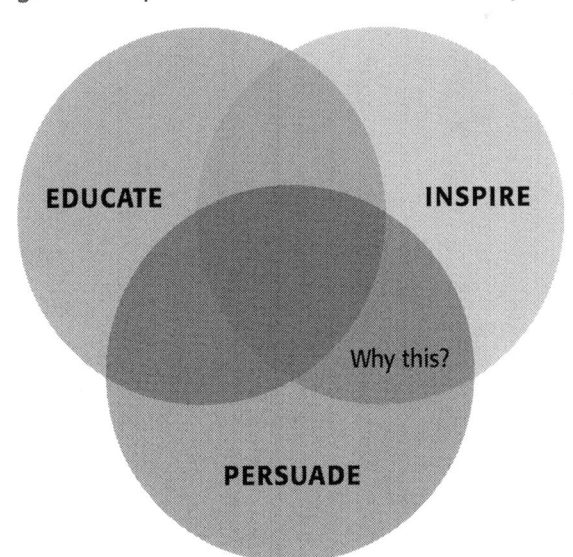

EDUCATE

INSPIRE

Why this?

PERSUADE

Consider the example of a motivational speaker. They may be able to whip up your feelings and give you great reasons to persuade you to take action to make changes to your life. But if their core message wasn't strong enough to compel you to make a lasting change (i.e., *"why should I do this?"*), then it's likely to quickly become irrelevant. And then you are far less likely to do anything different.

In this scenario, if you inspire and persuade but you don't educate adequately enough, you won't get the results you want.

"WHY YOU?"

If you only educate and persuade your audience, but don't adequately explain why they should feel like you're the one who can help them shed light on or solve the issue they're facing, they may ask, *"Why you?"* (See Figure 3.) In other words, *"Why should I trust you as the person who can guide me through this situation?"*

Figure 3: Educate + Persuade − Inspire = Why You?

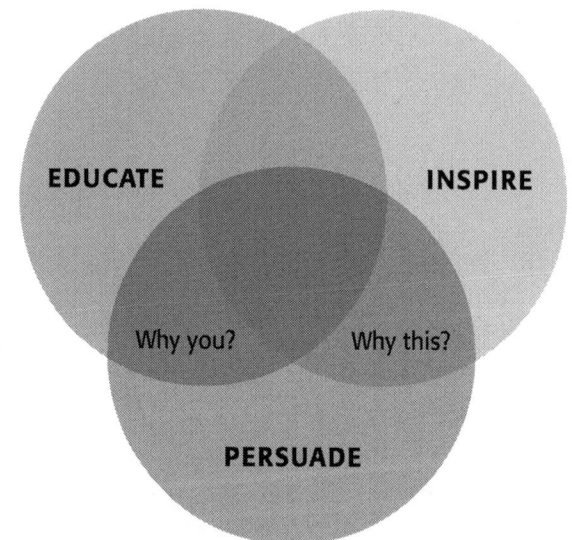

The best example of this scenario is a typical sales pitch. A salesperson walks into a technology company with a product that will revolutionize their next service offering. The IT company may be intrigued by the new offering and all the cool bells and whistles (educate), and want to move forward to add it to their next service offering (persuade). But if the salesperson wasn't able to build the connection and trust required to successfully make them feel like her solution is the best one for them and therefore *want* (inspire) to work directly with her, it's altogether possible that the company may choose to check out the competition, procrastinate on the decision, or try to get it cheaper from another source.

In this scenario, if you only educate and persuade but you don't inspire adequately enough, you won't get the results you want.

"WHY NOW?"

If you educate and inspire your audience, but don't provide them with specific actions to take and reasons why these actions need to be taken right away, they may ask, *"Why now?"* (See Figure 4).

Your audience may learn new information and feel like it would be worthwhile to do something, but without a specific plan of action, or internalizing why they need to take action, there would be no urgency or immediate need for them to actually do it *now*. And chances are that if they don't feel the urgency to take action now, then it becomes less and less likely to happen in the future as well.

For example, think of a doctor telling a patient why she should cut down on sugar. He may educate the patient on why sugar needs to be minimized and share lots of factual information that points to how likely it is that her health will improve by cutting it out of her diet. The patient might understand why it's important for her health to reduce her sugar consumption. She may be inspired to make these changes that he's suggesting, because she wants to take care of herself.

But, if the doctor can't give her an action plan to cut down on her late-night snacking, can't direct her to healthy substitutes when she's craving chocolate, and can't give her any tools to use when her will-power is low and she wants to reach for that second cupcake, then she ultimately won't do what needs to be done to cut out the sugar. And like so many of us sugary snack lovers (I'm raising my hand here!), those cookies will continue to hold lots of delicious, sugary power over her, and she will not follow through on the actions that she needs to take.

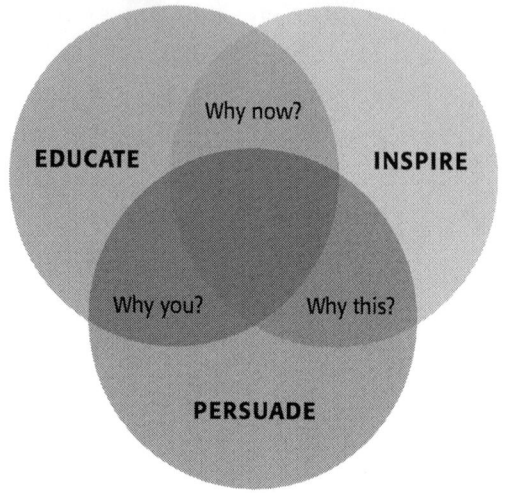

Figure 4: Educate + Inspire − Persuade = Why Now?

The bottom line is, if you educate and inspire but you aren't able to persuade well enough, you won't get the results you want.

NAILING THE KILLER PRESENTATION

But when you're clear on your essential message, and ensure that the content is crafted to educate, inspire, *and* persuade every time you give a presentation, then congratulations – you nailed it! (See Figure 5.)

Figure 5: Educate + Inspire + Persuade = Nailed It!

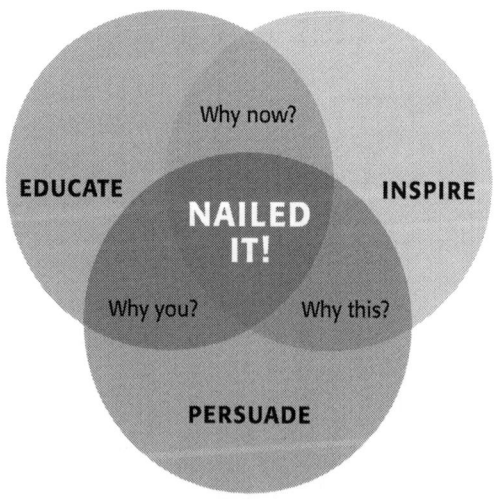

And when you educate, inspire *and* persuade – then congratulations again! You have delivered a true Killer Presentation, and can look forward to achieving the speaking results that you want.

 ## The Audience that Ran Away (Or the Case of the Super Successful and Super Boring Real Estate Agent)

A few years ago, I attended a networking group meeting where the organizers regularly gave a member 20 minutes to present themselves and what they do. On this particular night, a real estate agent was given this opportunity. And from the looks of it, she was a very successful one. Her hair was perfectly coiffed, she wore an expensive suit, tons of pearls, and the real symbol of success – killer shoes. She had a reputation of great experience and success in her chosen career, and we were looking forward to learning something new and relevant about the real estate industry.

Given that this was a networking meeting, I made the natural assumption of what kind of results she would want to achieve from her presentation: getting referrals, receiving information requests for future opportunities, and being "top of mind" as a leading real estate agent.

When the time came for her to start her presentation, she loaded up her slides, took her position in front of her audience, and smiled a big, confident smile.

And then, for the next 20 minutes, she made the worst mistake a speaker could ever make.

She did nothing but talk *only* about herself.

Her accomplishments, *her* awards, *her* wealth of experience, *her* income level, how *she* chose her real estate agency, the wonderful school *she* went to – and here's where it got really fascinating – what *all* the initials after her name meant.

As I looked around the room, the expression on everyone's faces was a mix of frustration, boredom, and something that I like to describe as "let me outta here!"

They were looking at their phones, shifting in their seats, and making eye contact with their colleagues with exasperated expressions.

At the end of her presentation, did *anyone* come up to her to ask for help in buying or selling their house? Did *anyone* give her any referrals? Did *anyone* even ask for more information?

Nope! Nada! Nothing!

In fact, at the end of her 20 minutes, we couldn't get out of there fast enough.

Do you think that she got the results she was hoping for?

Again, I say, nope!

And here's why. She was way too focused on what *she* wanted to say, and not at all on what *the audience* needed to hear.

Having been a member of that audience, it's safe to say that many of us would have been more interested in learning something more relevant to our own personal situations. Perhaps some industry news; what are interest rates like; tips for home staging; or how would we know when the markets are favorable to buy or sell our homes.

She could have inspired us to think of what our dream home could look like; how to choose the right agent; tips on getting a mortgage; working with moving companies; what to avoid when choosing an agent; future trends in real estate. She could even have shared examples and stories of other satisfied clients and how she had helped them in easy and pleasant real estate transactions.

Topics like those would have been far more interesting and meaningful than 20 minutes of credentials, an endless list of how many listings she holds, and how many houses she sells in a month.

She spoke in a very presenter-centric way, talking about what *she* wanted us to know, and seemed so sure that her qualifications and me-me-me content would dazzle us that she lost sight of what *we* could have actually learned from her extensive knowledge and expertise in this field.

And because she was so focused on what she wanted to say, and not what the audience needed to hear, she didn't create a *connection* with her audience.

And what do we know? Without connection, there's no trust; if there's no trust, there's no influence; no influence equals no results.

When your presentation is crafted in a way that educates, inspires, and persuades your audience, you are far more likely to achieve the speaking results that you want.

"The best way to sound like you know what you're talking about is to know what you're talking about."

AUTHOR UNKNOWN

The Next Step in Your Speaking Success: Structure

Now you're clear on what you want to say to your audience.

You're clear on what message your audience needs to hear so that it's relevant, meaningful, and valuable to them.

It's now time to turn our attention to the final – and critical – element in the Signature System. Let's now dive into how to piece together all the parts of your presentation into a rock-solid structure that not only captivates your audience and delivers huge value, but positions you as a leader – every time you speak.

CHAPTER 4

Your Secret Weapon for All Your Presentations: Structure

> "IF YOU CAN'T WRITE YOUR
> MESSAGE IN A SENTENCE, YOU
> CAN'T SAY IT IN AN HOUR."
>
> *Diana Booher*

Your Speaking Success System – Structure!

Whether you're new to speaking or you're a polished professional, your presentations need the same fundamental ingredient – Structure.

Clear, rock-solid, your-audience-will-love-you-for-it structure.

In the previous chapter, we discussed how to get clear on your essential message and position it in a way that is meaningful and relevant to your audience. Crafting your content in a way that educates, inspires, and persuades your audience is key to reaching that goal and building a Killer Presentation.

So now that you know *what* to say, strong speech structure will show you *how* to put it all together.

 Whether you're new to speaking or you're a seasoned professional, your presentations need the same fundamental ingredient – Structure.

Why is this so important? I've said it before, and I'll say it again. If there's no structure, it won't be clear. If it's not clear, the audience won't follow. If the audience doesn't follow, there's no value. And if there's no value, what's the point?

In her book *Resonate*,[4] presentation design expert Nancy Duarte talks about how a well-structured speech leads the audience on a journey. She likens it to a roller coaster with highs and lows, taking the audience to unexpected places through stories and examples, places where they can see themselves, and really connect with you and what you're saying.

Now that you know ***what*** *to say, strong speech structure will show you* ***how*** *to put it together.*

It's an art, it's a science, and it's all about creating connection and delivering value to the audience.

EXPERIENCED VS. BRAND-NEW SPEAKERS

Do you know what distinguishes an experienced speaker from a new one? Hint: You may be surprised.

I'll give you a moment to think about it.

OK, time's up.

The one thing that distinguishes an experienced speaker from a new one is … Nothing!

That's right. Nothing.

Killer Presentations don't depend on confidence, smooth delivery, or cool slides. They don't depend on good body language, how your voice carries, or intense eye contact.

Killer Presentations depend on *structure*.

- Structured content that is organized in a way that allows the audience to easily follow your message.

- Structured content that is crafted in a way that is interesting, engaging, and valuable to your audience.

- Structured content that is delivered with confidence, authenticity, and style, and that ensures you connect with your audience every step of the way.

- Structured content that flows fluidly in your speech through practice and rehearsal.

Experienced presenters know that a strong structure will not only make their message clear to their audience but will make it easier for them to present it as well. I've attended workshops in the past with professional speakers who get paid big money to speak, but who didn't have a structure, a point, or even a logical flow. At the same time, I've attended free workshops by relative unknowns, who deliver immense value that is structured so clearly that it literally changed my business and my life.

With a focused structure, a new speaker can be just as good as an experienced one.

ISN'T THE BASIC INTRODUCTION-BODY-CONCLUSION STRUCTURE ENOUGH?

Speech structure is based on the basic introduction-body-conclusion framework. But to really lead the audience on a journey, speech structure needs to go deeper and expand on what essential elements need to be included in the introduction, the body, and the conclusion to make your message far more relevant and engaging.

 The success of any presentation relies on strong, relevant content built into a focused structure.

The structure relies on the strength of your content, and how it is built into a focused, engaging, and compelling presentation that is both meaningful and valuable to an audience.

Now that we understand that, here comes the fun part!

CLARITY IS KEY

To craft a Killer Presentation, you also need clarity on:

- Your essential message;
- Who your audience is and what they need to hear; and

- How to craft your content so that you can educate, inspire, and persuade your audience.

Clarity within your focused speech structure is an absolute must. It will allow you to share valuable content that is easy for your audience to follow, for you to deliver, and that positions you as a trusted leader.

Now it's time to make it happen, using an incredibly effective tool that will help you create this structure easily, quickly, and effectively.

Enter ... The Diamond Speech Structure Flowchart

The Diamond Speech Structure Flowchart™ (see Figure 6) – hereafter referred to as "The Diamond" – is the one tool that will forever change how you create your presentations.

It gives you a clear, concise, powerful structure that's logical and easy to follow – both for you as a speaker when you're crafting the speech, and for your audience, when they're listening to it.

The Diamond helps you:

- Define the best type of content that needs to be "plugged in," while always keeping sight of the value it's giving the audience.

- Find all the ways to grab audience attention in a Strong Introduction, how to set the speech objective, and how to flesh out your Key Points.

- Integrate the right stories at the right time in the speech, and how to use these stories in ways that truly captivate the audience.

- Identify how to master transitions from one point to another, how and where in the speech to compel your audience to take action, and how to end with impact.

- Elevate your credibility, visibility, and trust with your audience – whether it's a sales team, a whole company, a group of investors, a roomful of conference attendees, or even an audience of one, like the one key client, manager, or stakeholder who can really make a difference to your career or business.

The first few times that I used it with my coaching clients, it was something so powerful that even the clients were a little taken aback at how simple – and effective – it was to create a presentation. It helped them reflect on what was missing in previous presentations and shed light on how to make future presentations more successful. It was an incredibly useful tool to help filter their ideas and manage the overwhelming feelings they so commonly experienced when trying to determine what content to put into their presentations. After a couple of sessions, it became easy for them to move forward to create multiple speeches quickly, easily, effectively – and completely on their own.

Once they started using this speech structure framework, building their presentations with it, getting out in front of audiences and totally *nailing* it – getting the great feedback, the sales, the requests for meetings, the recognition from colleagues and clients, and the range of other results that they were after – we all knew that it was big!

 The Diamond Speech Structure Flowchart will forever change how you create structure into your presentations. Try it the next time you have to present!

TAKE THE "MESS" OUT OF YOUR MESSAGE

In the initial stages of creating a presentation, it's natural to have lots of ideas of what content needs to be included into the presentation. This is where we brainstorm, we outline, and we put all our ideas on the table. Some of us organize using sticky notes, mind maps, or long lists. There is no one right way to do this, and the best guideline is to follow the style that works effectively for you.

There's no doubt that this process can sometimes get messy. With so many ideas, information, and, often, other people's opinions being added to the mix, it can be a challenge to decide exactly what content makes it into the final presentation. And that's OK. Brainstorm, collect all your ideas, stories, and examples onto one document, whiteboard, spreadsheet, or master list. Once everything is in one place, you'll likely get a clearer picture of what you're working with, and how to integrate it into your speech structure.

And that's exactly when you would pull out the Diamond to help your presentation take shape through a defined, focused, and engaging speech structure.

It's OK to be "messy" when crafting your presentation. Put all your ideas "on the table." When you can see all of your ideas in one place, it becomes easier to organize them and choose the most relevant content.

Figure 6: The Diamond Speech Structure Flowchart

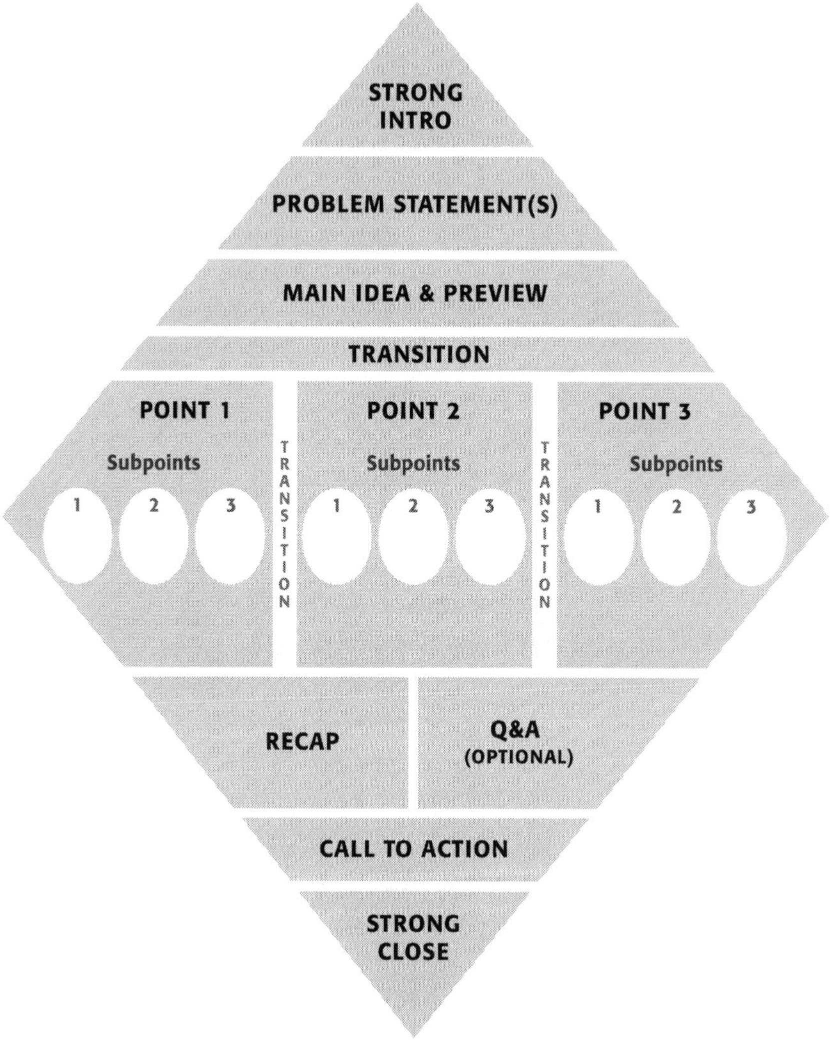

STRONG INTRO

PROBLEM STATEMENT(S)

MAIN IDEA & PREVIEW

TRANSITION

POINT 1

Subpoints

1 2 3

TRANSITION

POINT 2

Subpoints

1 2 3

TRANSITION

POINT 3

Subpoints

1 2 3

RECAP

Q&A (OPTIONAL)

CALL TO ACTION

STRONG CLOSE

TWO IMPORTANT STEPS BEFORE YOU DIVE INTO THE DIAMOND

There are two key steps that must be addressed well before you start thinking about applying the Diamond to structure your presentation.

1. **Get Clear on Your Objective.** In Chapter 3, we discussed how it's important to think carefully about what you need to say to educate, inspire, and persuade your audience. What do you want them to learn, feel, and do as a result of hearing your presentation? Remember that this objective must be established *before* you begin creating your content. It must also be revisited throughout your presentation to make sure you – and your message – stay on track.

   Your objective is *not* about making a sale or booking a meeting. There's a place for that in the Call-to-Action segment of your presentation. At this stage, your purpose is to reflect only on the essential message that you want them to get from your presentation.

   Let's be clear here. Building your structure cannot proceed without clarity on the objective.

2. **Understand Your Audience.** Who is in your audience? Why are they there? Are they required to be there, or do they choose to be there? What do they already know about your topic? What questions are they likely to ask? What does a day in their life look like? What issues or challenges are they dealing with that have resulted in them being in your audience, or in your meeting, or having this conversation with you? And how do these issues or challenges affect them on a day-to-day basis? Addressing these realities – and ensuring that the content speaks to it – will make a meaningful difference in how well and how quickly you are able to engage and connect with your audience.

The goal is for your audience to say, "Hey, she really gets it. She gets *me*."

When your audience feels that way, then you know that connection has been made.

NAILED IT! Before starting to craft your presentation, it's important to have clarity on two items: 1. The objective of your presentation; and 2. Your audience's needs, wants, and challenges. This will help you create more relevant, actionable content.

STICK TO YOUR OBJECTIVE (YOU CAN DO IT!)

You need to check in with your objective at every step of your speech, and make sure that your content keeps it in mind. For example, a financial advisor's objective may be to educate her clients of all the different ways that they can save for retirement, inspire them to want to save, to persuade them to be more active in planning their financial future by considering the services of a financial advisor. This objective is very audience-focused, and still offers the opportunity for the financial advisor to pitch her services in the Call-to-Action segment of the Diamond. However, the purpose must always be communicated from the point of view of how it benefits and provides value to the audience.

The Diamond – in Detail

Now that you're clear on your objective, you can jump into the Diamond and move step-by-step through crafting your structured, easy-to-follow, compelling presentation.

The Diamond is divided into three main segments, which remain consistent with the core elements of speech structure – that is, the Introduction, Body, and Conclusion. Within each of these elements, we'll drill down to the specific pieces necessary to really make your presentation – and you – stand out.

1. **Introduction:** This section is made up of the Strong Intro, the Problem Statement, and the Main Idea and Preview. The Transition starts here, and re-appears in several other areas in the Diamond.

2. **Body:** This section includes Key Points and the Sub-Points.

3. **Conclusion:** This section includes the Recap, Q&A, Call-to-Action, and Strong Close.

The Speech Introduction

The Speech Introduction = Strong Intro + Problem Statement +
Main Idea & Preview + Transition

The primary goals of a speech Introduction – whether it's for a persuasive speech or an informative one – are to:

- Establish the topic and purpose of the presentation;
- Introduce yourself and why you're uniquely qualified to be speaking about this topic; and
- Take hold of the audience's curiosity and concentration.

A good Introduction grabs your audience's attention from the start and establishes the reason they would *want* to listen to you.

The top third of the Diamond (see Figure 7) represents the full Introduction, which includes the:

- Strong Intro;
- Problem Statement;
- Main Idea and Preview; and
- Transition #1.

 A good Introduction grabs your audience's attention right away, addresses their needs, and establishes the reason they would *want* to listen to you.

1. STRONG INTRO

The Strong Intro is the warm-up, the enticement, the moment where you need to establish connection and grab their attention fast. You can do it with a story, a question, an unexpected statement, a bold claim. In a corporate setting, however, you may want to skip the warm-up, and go straight to the purpose of the meeting.

"You had me at 'Hello.'"

RENÉE ZELLWEGER AS DOROTHY BOYD
IN *JERRY MAGUIRE*

Figure 7: The Diamond Speech Structure Flowchart – The Introduction

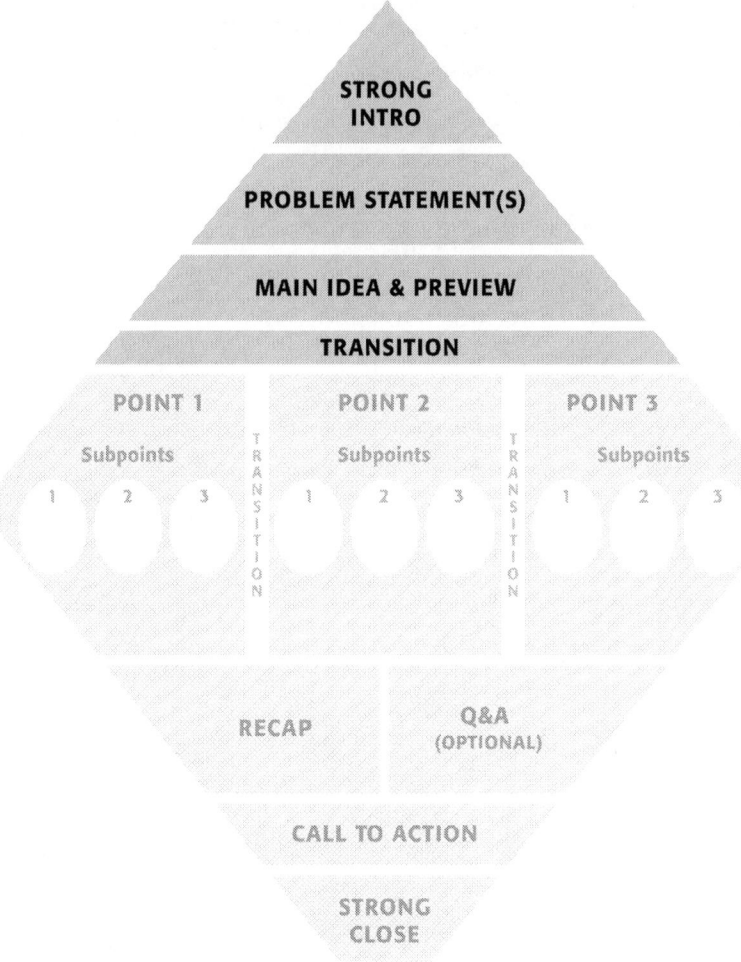

Here are some ideas on how *not* to start a speech.

- "I'm a bit nervous, bear with me."
- "This is my first time speaking to a group this big."
- "My name is …" (If you've been introduced, we already know your name.)
- "Today I want to talk about …" (Don't start your speech in the middle. Your audience needs a warm-up.)

- "Crazy weather we've been having …"

Start with value, not filler.

The Strong Intro is important to quickly engage the audience within the first few seconds of when you start speaking by establishing a reason or motivation for listening to the presentation.

2. PROBLEM STATEMENT

The Problem Statement encourages you to address the purpose, or the "why?" of the presentation. Very often, this is reflected in a problem, issue, update, or challenge that you know your audience is dealing with, or a problem that exists that you – and the content in your presentation – can solve. It establishes the purpose of the presentation and is where you would be creating a connection with your audience.

In a corporate setting, the Problem Statement and the Strong Intro often work hand-in-hand, because presentations may start directly with addressing the problem or issue facing a team so that they understand why the presentation is relevant to them.

The Problem Statement addresses these three very key questions that *every* audience is asking as they listen to you speak:

1. "So what?"
2. "Why is this important to me?"
3. "Why should I care?"

If you can answer those three questions within the first two minutes of your speech, your ability to connect with your audience – and the potential for the success of your presentation – will skyrocket.

The Problem Statement is important because it is where you show your listeners that you understand their current situation, that you "get" them, and assures them that you're going to share tools, ideas, and strategies that will be useful for them to move forward.

> *"I've learned that people will forget what you said,*
> *people will forget what you did, but people will*
> *never forget how you made them feel."*
>
> MAYA ANGELOU

3. THE MAIN IDEA AND PREVIEW

The Main Idea focuses the audience on the essential message of your presentation, and the Preview shares a brief overview of the Key Points you'll be expanding on in the Body of the speech.

While the Main Idea and Preview are closely linked, they will both be addressed separately, for clarification.

The Main Idea

The Main Idea is a *one-sentence description* of the main premise or intention of your presentation. Getting clear on the Main Idea will help both you and your audience stay focused on the core message.

Let's break it down. The Main Idea addresses:

- *Who* you're speaking to;
- *What* you'll be speaking about; and
- *Why* it's important to them.

The Main Idea might look like this:

> My intention in this presentation is to share/show/prove how …
>
> Every _____ can _____ so that [they can] _____
>   *(who)*   *(what)*   *(why)*

You can even get creative and reverse the order of the *who*, the *what* and the *why*. Here are some examples.

> My intention in the next half hour is to share how every entrepreneur in this room (*who*) can create and deliver a structured, engaging speech (*what*), so that every time they speak, they stand out as a leader (*why*).

> My intention in this presentation is to share with you (*who*) how our products address the needs of your target market (*what*), so that they know to call *you* the next time this need arises (*why*).

> My intention is to share news and updates on our project (*what*), so that everyone in this room (*who*) understands their role in getting this product update launched on time, on budget, and ready for our clients (*why*).

The Main Idea is important because, after whatever facts, information, challenges, or stories you've addressed during the Speech Intro and Problem Statement, it re-focuses the audience on the essential message. It reiterates what the main topic of the presentation will be – and why it will be relevant to them – before moving into the Body of the speech.

The Main Idea is also important because when you're clear on your Main Idea while you're crafting your presentation, it will keep you focused on building the right content through the rest of the process.

The Preview

The Preview provides a high-level introduction of the key concepts, first referred to in the Main Idea, that you'll be talking about throughout your presentation. These will eventually be uncovered in more detail in the Key Points of your presentation, which are the core elements in the Body of the presentation.

If it's the Main Idea that sets up the *who*, *what*, and *why*, it's the Preview that sets up the *how*. And when you've got those four elements covered, then you've really helped yourself get clear on how to build your presentation, and you've helped your audience get clear on what value they'll be receiving.

> *The Main Idea sets up the **who**, **what**, and **why**; the Preview sets up the **how**.*

Here's an example for putting these two parts together.

Main Idea: My intention in the next half hour is to share how every entrepreneur in this room (*who*) can create and deliver a structured, engaging speech (*what*), so that every time they speak, they stand out as a leader (*why*).

Preview: To do this, I'll be covering:

1. How to get clear on the main objective of your presentation.
2. How to structure your presentation using the Diamond Speech Structure Framework.
3. How to deliver the presentation with confidence and ease.

> **Main Idea:** My intention in this presentation is to share with you (*who*) how our products address the needs of your target market (*what*), so that they know to call you the next time this need arises (*why*).
>
> **Preview:** To do this, we're going to talk about:
> 1. The makeup and general needs of our target market.
> 2. Our product's features and benefits.
> 3. Sales strategies and ideas.

> **Main Idea:** My intention is to share news and updates on our project (*what*), so that everyone in this room (*who*) understands their role in getting this product update launched on time, on budget, and ready for our clients (*why*).
>
> **Preview:** So I will cover:
> 1. Project status updates.
> 2. Current challenges, opportunities, and customer feedback.
> 3. Next steps.

Sometimes you may have a lot of information that you'd like to share in the presentation. Therefore, the points that you choose in the Preview should be limited to those that directly address the *what* and the *why* of the Main Idea, as well as the issues or challenges brought up in the Problem Statement. Some helpful tips on how to narrow down your focus to choose the right points are provided in the section on Key Points.

The Preview is important because it gives your audience a sneak peek of the core content of the presentation.

4. THE TRANSITION

The Transition is how you clearly and smoothly move from one idea to the next. It is used throughout the entire speech, when preparing to introduce a new concept or idea. The Transition itself, however, does not introduce new content.

On the Diamond, you'll see the Transition in three places – right before, and then between the introduction of the Key Points and Sub-Points. However, Transitions occur anywhere in the speech where you're moving from one idea to the next.

There are several ways to use Transitions effectively. Consider any of the options listed below.

1. Silence/Pause between points.

2. Numbering it off. Example: "This brings us to our third point ..."

3. Changing the time span. "Four years later, I found myself in a new situation ..."

4. Movement. This is most useful if you're on a stage, or in the front of a meeting room, a boardroom, or a classroom, as you can move over to another side of the stage or room to start a new topic.

5. Visuals. Showing different images or designs in your slides signifies a change in content direction.

6. Verbal cues, like, "Speaking of ..." or "Any questions on this part?" or "In light of that, the next thing that is important to address is ..."

It's best to vary your Transition techniques throughout the speech to keep it interesting for the audience.

The Transition is important because it allows for better speech flow and a logical, smooth movement from one point to the next.

And that is your basic speech Introduction expanded into the Diamond!

The Strong Intro, Problem Statement, Main Idea and Preview, and Transition are all part of the overall speech Introduction. It shows how, when you dig deep into expanding the introductory content, all the pieces can work together to build something very meaningful. Now it's time to move to the middle, or Body, of the speech.

The Body of the Speech

The Body of the Speech = The Key Points + The Sub-Points

The Body of your speech is where you spend most of your time in the presentation. This is where you'll be educating your audience with the information, facts, stories, statistics, updates, examples, and details that address the realities that you brought up in the Problem Statement and continued in the Main Idea and the Preview.

Figure 8: The Diamond Speech Structure Flowchart – The Body

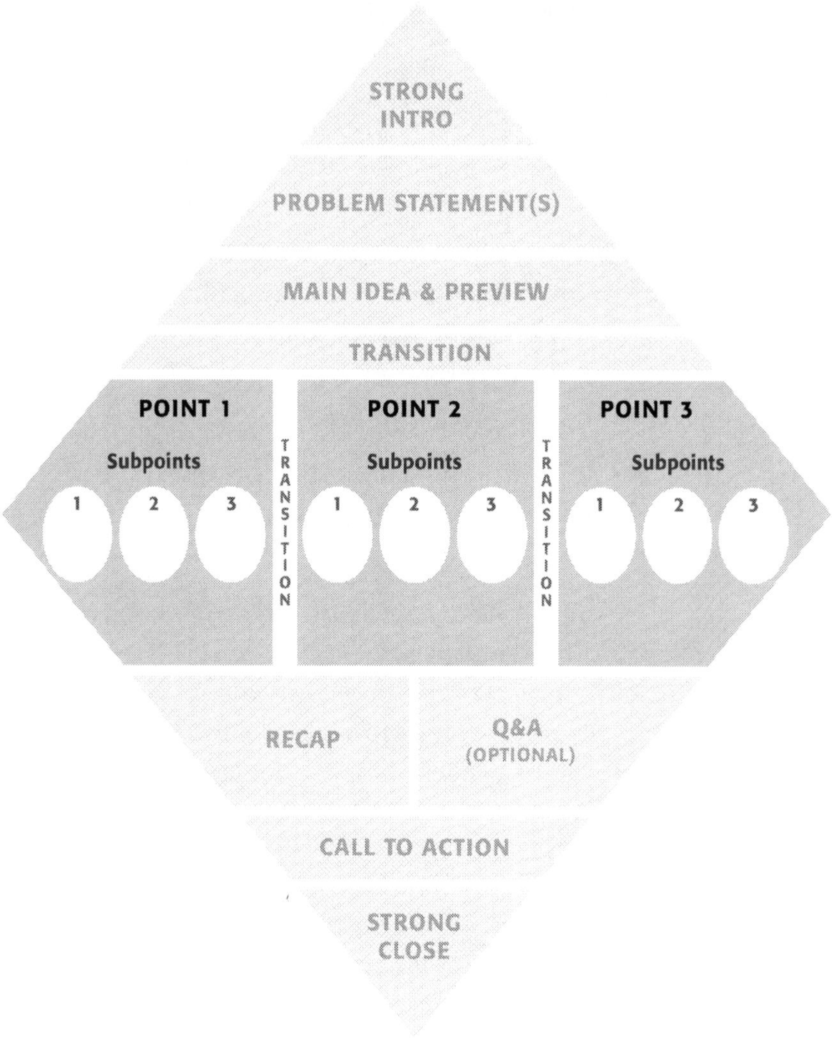

STRONG
INTRO

PROBLEM STATEMENT(S)

MAIN IDEA & PREVIEW

TRANSITION

POINT 1			T R A N S I T I O N	POINT 2			T R A N S I T I O N	POINT 3		
Subpoints				Subpoints				Subpoints		
1	2	3		1	2	3		1	2	3

RECAP

Q&A
(OPTIONAL)

CALL TO ACTION

STRONG
CLOSE

The two elements of the Diamond that address the Body of your speech are the Key Points and the Sub-Points (see Figure 8).

 The Key Points and Sub-Points *educate* the audience with information, facts, stories, statistics, updates, examples, and other relevant details.

5. KEY POINTS

The Key Points are a direct extension of the information you talked about in your Preview, but now will be addressed in greater detail in the speech. For example, in the Preview, when you say "Here are the three ideas that I'm going to talk about," well, the Key Points are where you start talking about them in more depth.

It is in the Sub-Points category where you would dive into your content. The Sub-Points share the information – those facts, stories, statistics, updates, examples, and details – that make up each Key Point. Essentially, all the ideas that you're using to educate your audience are in this section.

With that in mind, how do you filter down all this information to decide *which* points make it to your final presentation?

Focus, Focus, Focus!

Start by creating the full list of what you feel is relevant to talk about in your presentation. Then go through this list and narrow down the points that specifically address the issues brought up in the Problem Statement. Since part of your objective is to get very clear on understanding your audience, it's often helpful to put yourself in their shoes and ask yourself, "So what? Why is this important to me? Why should I care?" These answers should give you some insights to help you decide what information is most relevant to put into the presentation.

Second, consider that the other part of your objective is to educate, inspire, and persuade your audience. You want them to learn something new, perhaps change a behavior or way of thinking, buy into an idea, take an action. Here again, you can ask yourself, "What do I want my audience to learn, feel, and do as a result of my presentation?" Look at your Key Points from that perspective to help you choose the right content to put into the presentation.

Finally, consider which ideas you can develop more deeply, which you have the most information about, and which ones are most likely to engage your audience.

The Powerful "Rule of Three"

The Rule of Three states that it's generally best to choose three Key Points to share with your audience, simply because three points are easier for them to digest and remember. This isn't to say that you can *never* have more than three points, however, giving your audience more than four or five points may run the risk of overwhelming them with too much information.

> *"Using the Rule of three allows you to express concepts more completely, emphasize your points, and increase the memorability of your message."*
>
> ANDREW DLUGAN

The good news is that if you do have a lot of information to cover, there is some flexibility in the Diamond that allows you to structure each of your Key Points in a way that includes more than three points.

When you have determined all of that, you can then move onto building your Sub-Points.

The Key Points are important because they give your audience a structured, focused view into the core content of the presentation.

6. SUB-POINTS

The Sub-Points are represented by three circles under each Key Point (see Figure 8). This section of the Diamond is intended to guide you in providing the content that makes up your Key Points in a variety of informational or even creative ways.

Of course, there can be exceptions to the rule. Some presentations may not necessarily need exactly three Sub-Points within each Key Point. Maybe for one Key Point there is only one piece of relevant information to share, and therefore only one Sub-Point is used. Or you may have four ideas to communicate. That's fine, as long as you keep it clear and focused.

Don't Let the Facts Ruin Your Presentation

When populating our Sub-Points, the first thing that most of us will do is to focus on conveying the facts. This, of course, is a great starting point. However, if you fill your presentation *only* with facts, and not stories, relevant examples, or actions that your listeners should take, you will be educating your audience, but you may miss out on the opportunity to inspire and persuade them as well.

In Nancy Duarte's book, *Resonate*, she has this to say about facts.[5]

> Facts are one type of content to collect, but they're not the only type needed to create a successful presentation. You must strike a balance between analytical and emotional content. ... Stating fact after fact in an hour-long presentation doesn't signal to the audience *why* these facts are important. Staying flat and factual might work in a scientific report, but simply won't work for the oral delivery of persuasive content.

Consider using some of the examples below to make your facts more engaging to your audience.

- Stories (more on this in Chapter 5)
- Examples
- Current events/news
- Visuals, like images and videos – Just be aware of the copyright rules for stock photos or videos if you intend to use them in a presentation. Or get creative and use your own photos where possible. You may find that giving a snapshot into your own life can add a greater level of connection and personalization with your audience.
- Interviews
- Analogies/metaphors – A comparison made to show a similarity. (E.g., "Life is a highway.")
- A rhyme, poem, or quote – Not recommended for business presentations, but can applicable in other contexts.
- Individual exercise – Asking your audience to do something specific. (E.g., "Take two minutes and write down the goals of your business.")
- Group exercises – Again, great for training or workshops, less

suitable for corporate presentations. (E.g., "Turn to the person next to you and share ...")

- In most virtual presentation platforms, there are multiple ways to create interaction and engagement with your audience. Some examples include running polls, asking audience members to interact via the chat functions, creating opportunities for movement or putting your audience into breakout rooms if you want them to participate in smaller group discussions or exercises.

The Sub-Points are important because you can use a variety of engaging speaking techniques to back up your essential message, which will then allow you to educate, inspire, and persuade your audience throughout this whole section of your presentation.

> *"When anyone asks me 'how many*
> *speeches do you have?' I don't understand*
> *the question. I have 48 hours of good*
> *content that I pull from and organize*
> *into a speech for this audience."*
>
> ZIG ZIGLAR

The Speech Conclusion

The Conclusion = The Recap + Q&A + Call-to-Action + Strong Close

As critical as it is to start your presentation with impact so that you can capture your audience's attention and show why the presentation will be relevant for them, it's equally important to end it in a powerful way.

The purpose of the Conclusion is to summarize your Key Points, compel your audience to *do* something via a powerful Call-to-Action, and inspire them to visualize what their new reality might look like if they move forward with the concepts put forth in your presentation.

The bottom third of the Diamond (see Figure 9) represents the Conclusion.

In my training programs, workshops, and coaching, I have seen many clients give otherwise good presentations that seem to fall apart at the end. They present their Key Points, substantiated with their

Sub-Points, which is then followed by something like, "That's it, thank you," or "That's what I wanted to present to you today," or "Now go out there and make it happen."

Figure 9: The Diamond Speech Structure Flowchart – The Conclusion

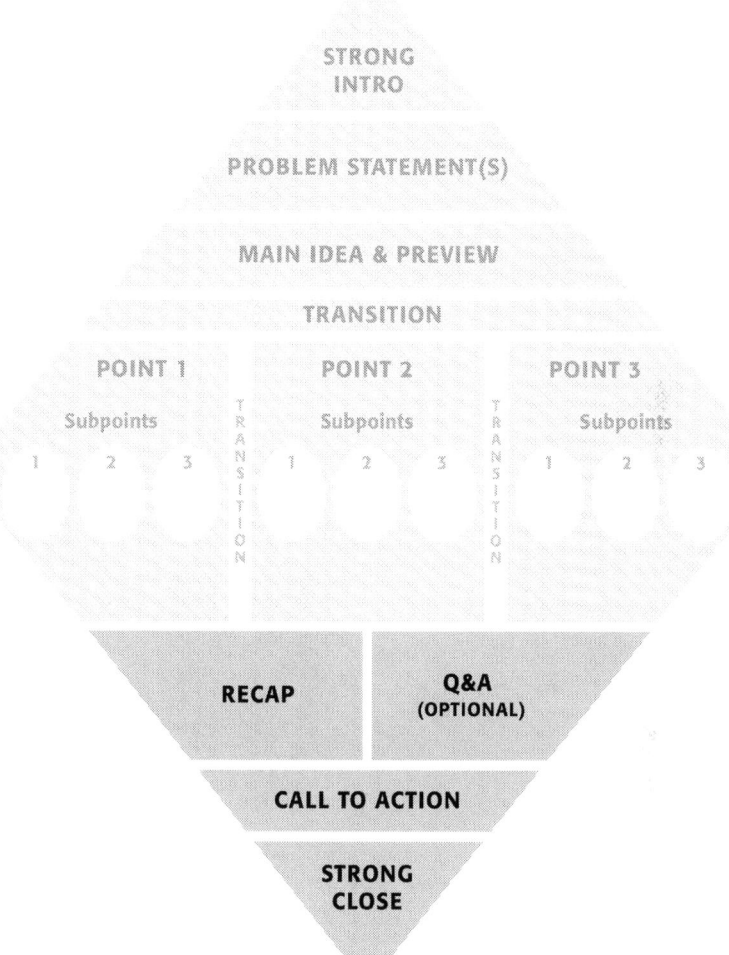

While you may want to finish your presentation and get it over with, remember that as a speaker, the Conclusion is your final chance to drive home your ideas, create impact, and compel action to get the results that you want. When a speaker provides a lackluster or weak Conclusion – or no Conclusion at all – the speech loses the energy that's been created, with the eventual result that the audience is left confused, indifferent, or frustrated.

Don't waste that opportunity. Plan ahead so that your Conclusion will be an impactful one.

 The Conclusion is your final chance to drive home your ideas, create impact, and compel your audience to action.

There are four critical components in the Diamond to concluding your presentation in an effective, powerful way. These are the:

- Recap;
- Q&A;
- Call-to-Action; and
- Strong Close.

7. THE RECAP

The Recap reminds your audience of your essential message, and may also include a recap of your Key Points, in order to reinforce what is most important for the audience to remember from your presentation.

The usefulness of the Recap is highlighted in the book, *Memory*,[6] by German psychologist Hermann Ebbinghaus. The author theorizes that an individual's ability to remember information in a list (e.g., a grocery list, a chores list, or a to-do list) depends on the location of an item on the list. Specifically, he found that items toward the top of the list and bottom of the list tended to have the highest recall rates. So, if we apply this concept to our presentations, this would mean that what you cover in the introduction and the conclusion of a presentation – in the Diamond, that would be the Strong Intro and the Strong Close – has a higher likelihood of being recalled by your audience than the information that you present in the middle, or the Body of your speech.

In 1945, Ray Ehrensberger tested this theory as it relates to public speaking and found that the information delivered during the Conclusion had the highest level of recall overall.[7]

Based on that, it's easy to see why we must put a lot of thought into our Conclusion, so that we, as speakers, can ensure that the audience recalls the most significant points.

There are two different elements in an effective Recap.

1. **Restate the Main Idea of the Speech.** This reminds the audience of the purpose or intent of the speech, and re-emphasizes its essential message.

2. **Restate the Key Points of the Speech.** This highlights the importance of the Key Points and increases the likelihood that the audience will retain them after the speech is over.

The Recap is important because it helps to clarify the essential elements of a speech in the quickest way possible.

 When we preview our main points in the Introduction, discuss them in greater detail in the Body of the speech, and recap them in the Conclusion, we increase the likelihood that the audience will retain these points after the speech is over.

8. Q&A

The Q&A is the Question-and-Answer period of a presentation. Depending on where you're delivering your presentation – be it in a boardroom, a zoom call, or a conference – you may stop at different intervals of your speech to take questions, you may be interrupted with questions, or you may leave all questions to the end.

On the Diamond, the Q&A is listed as optional, because not every presentation will incorporate a formal Q&A.

Why Isn't the Q&A at the End of the Presentation?

I have always believed that Q&A sessions should *not* be the final words of a presentation. That honor should be reserved for the Strong Close, which leaves the audience with the inspiring words that compel them to leave your presentation more educated, inspired, and persuaded to take action. Replacing that important end spot of a presentation with a Q&A can take away the opportunity to end with the impact you intended.

Consider a few of the different scenarios that can occur during a Q&A session.

- You get a question ... and it's a good question, and you answer it. This is the best-case scenario.

- There are no questions. So, there you are, awkwardly waiting and hoping for a question.

- You get asked a question ... and it's not a very relevant one. "Can you repeat the definition of a term?" "What did it say on slide four?" "Will these slides be available afterwards?" Perfectly valid questions, but probably not the ones you're hoping for to showcase your great expertise.

- You get a question ... and you don't know the answer. Yikes!

- You get a difficult question from an audience member who wants to debate something that you said or share their very extensive opinion about it. This has the potential to frustrate the rest of your audience and eat into the rest of your speech time. You don't necessarily want to get into a debate about your well thought-out, prepared content in the final moments of your speech, as these are the moments that are most critical for your audience to reflect on your final, impactful points – and not to get sidetracked by a distracting discussion.

The Q&A is the one part of the speech where you simply can't predict what will happen. If it doesn't go well, or if it goes just OK, or even if the questions are great, that's not the final message that you want your audience to remember. You want to end your presentation with what you have meticulously planned for them to retain and remember.

Ultimately, in some presentations it won't be possible to plan for questions to come exactly when you want them to. And in some organizations, the culture may be one where there is an open Q&A throughout, or at the end of a presentation. As a best practice, however, the Q&A *after* the Recap and *before* the Strong Close is effective because it allows you to finish your speech the way you have prepared it, with the formulated final words that you have carefully crafted to end with impact.

You're in a meeting presenting your status update, and things are going well. You're feeling good about your presentation, and the group seems reassured that you're on top of things. Then, just as you're about to finish up, someone in the room pipes up and asks you a question about one of the details that you presented – and you don't know the answer!

With all eyes on you, waiting for your response, what do you do?

Your first reaction may be to give the honest answer, and just say, "I don't know."

Here's why you *don't* want to say that.

Simply put, saying "I don't know" costs you credibility and influence.

Saying "I don't know" teaches people not to come to *you* for answers next time.

And think of how awkward it is for you to be put on the spot and admit that you don't know an answer after you've prepared a presentation about that topic. That could really affect your confidence and credibility going forward.

Here are three alternative, much more powerful responses than "I don't know," which will keep your credibility, confidence, and authority intact.

1. "I don't have enough information right now to answer your question. I will look into it and get back to you." And then follow through and get them that information.

2. "Good question. I'll find out." And then, find out.

3. "Based on what we know today, my thoughts are ..." And then share those thoughts.

While you never want to *guess* an answer, this response allows you a little leeway to at least share an educated opinion and buy yourself some time to get the full details.

> And of course, *always* follow up with the individual who asked the question. This will prove that you're true to your word. The next time that you're stumped in a Q&A session and asked a question that you're not able to answer, you can ditch "I don't know," and *still* respond with honesty in a way that builds your authority, your confidence, and your credibility.

"Last words linger."
PATRICIA FRIPP

9. CALL-TO-ACTION

An audience might be captivated by your message and thoroughly believe that what you're saying is right, but if they leave not knowing what they are supposed to do next, or how to implement your suggestions and ideas, then your presentation will have been – essentially – useless.

Enter the Call-to-Action.

A Call-to-Action is an explicit appeal to your audience to take a specific action following your speech. It should come right before the conclusion of a presentation, and it gives audience members concrete tasks to undertake that must be completed in order to bring your ideas to fruition.

How to move forward on a project, give the presentation, be more creative, exercise more, procrastinate less, manage their time better, invest in a company, speak up in a meeting, eat more vegetables, go after the promotion, attend an event, build an online course, read a book, write a book, sign a petition, train for a marathon, donate to a cause, and the list goes on and on. It could also include Calls-to-Action specific to what you want to sell, such as visit your website, get a free trial, subscribe now, register today, book you to deliver another speech, hire you as a consultant, get a referral, buy your products or services, book a call, schedule a meeting, or get a coffee together.

Your Call-to-Action and your approach to delivering it may vary according to your audience and your speaking style.

People respond to different types of Calls-to-Action based on their temperaments, communication needs, priorities, goals, and more. So first, get to know who is in your audience, and then customize a direct and specific Call-to-Action that makes the benefits of taking action very clear.

For example, try these options.

- Instead of saying "You might want to think about investing in this new program," try "Invest in this program, and here's how you'll start seeing the results immediately."

- Instead of "This is a good exercise program, take a look at it," say "Here's how you can start this exercise program today, so you don't have to wait any longer to prioritize your health."

- Instead of "This non-profit organization has a target of $10,000 for a new program that we can reach with your help," say "If you sign up right now to volunteer for one of our events, that will get us closer to helping those in need."

The Call-to-Action is important because it moves your audience to take action and *do something* so that they can move past whatever issue, challenge, problem, or reality they're currently facing (as stated in the Problem Statement).

10. THE STRONG CLOSE (AKA THE VISIONARY CONCLUSION)

The Strong Close ends a presentation with impact, meaning, and relevance. I also like to refer to it as a "Visionary Conclusion," because with it, you create a vision of the success that your audience might experience if they take your advice, implement your strategies, and/or do what you suggested they do. This is very different – and far more effective – from ending a presentation with the typical Conclusion of "So, that's it," "I'm done," or "Thank you."

Here are a few other effective ways to close a presentation.

- Revisit the anecdote, rhetorical statement, quotation, or opening you used in the Introduction – because your audience will surely see the question differently after your talk.

- Finish a story that you started somewhere in the speech.

- Firmly restate your basic Conclusion or recommendation.
- If you provided some kind of a future vision of what life could be like once they have addressed and overcome the problem, remind them of it.

The Strong Close should always refer to the original intention of what you wanted your audience to learn, feel or do by the end of your speech, and how doing what you're suggesting in this presentation will help them get there.

The Strong Close is important because it creates closure and a sense of finality to your speech.

The Perils of Ending with the Sales Pitch

If you choose to end your presentation with a Visionary Conclusion, you will create a vision of what your audience's life can be like if they follow your advice, recommendations, and expertise. Done well, it will leave your audience clear on your message, clear on the benefits of what you suggested, and feeling inspired and motivated to take action.

How might that change if you end your speech with a sales pitch? One possible risk is that *your* energy can change. You can go from being a strong, powerful speaker to feeling a bit reserved or awkward once you start asking for the sale. Not everyone is as confident when they go into "sales mode," and this can change the energy – and the outcome – of a Conclusion.

From the audience's perspective, there may be people who get turned off by a sales pitch, and then they leave your talk with the sales pitch in their mind, and *not* the inspiring, structured content, and strong Conclusion that you wanted them to leave with.

This doesn't mean, however, that there's no space for a sales pitch. Presenting your products or services in order to get more business is a key marketing strategy and can often be a very effective one as well. So, here's the easy fix: Put your Call-to-Action *before* your Conclusion, more specifically, after you've finished talking about all the Key Points, and before you go into your Strong Close.

Just as we need to ensure that the Q&A comes before our Strong Close, the same holds true for the Call-to-Action. If you've structured your Key Points – the Body of the speech – correctly, it should easily flow to the question of "How can we make this happen?" or "Where do we go from here?" Then, you can more easily turn attention towards sharing your products or services, or asking for a meeting. And after that's done, you go straight into your Strong Close, leaving your inspiring, impactful words as the last thing your audience hears.

 If you want to pitch your products or services, don't leave it to the end of your presentation. Put your Call-to-Action *before* your Conclusion. That way, your inspiring, impactful words – and *not* your sales pitch – will be the last thing your audience hears.

Using this method, even if your Call-to-Action and sales pitch don't go as wonderfully as you would have hoped, you can still redeem yourself by ending the presentation with the inspiring words that you want them to remember.

> *"It's not how strongly you feel about*
> *your topic, it's how strongly they feel*
> *about your topic after you speak."*
>
> TIM SALLADAY

Use the Diamond to Educate, Inspire, and Persuade

If you remember the essential components to building a Killer Presentation that were covered in Chapter 3 – who are we kidding, of course you remember! – then you'll know that they require you to:

- *Educate* your audience so that they *learn* what you want them to learn;
- *Inspire* your audience so that they *feel* what you want them to feel; and
- *Persuade* your audience so that they *do* what you want them to do.

While these components must be established prior to putting together your actual presentation, if you're following all the steps laid out in this book, you'll be able to see how each segment of the Diamond – categorized into the Introduction, Body and Conclusion – corresponds to all the steps in creating a Killer Presentation (see Figure 10).

Figure 10: The Diamond Speech Structure Flowchart and the Killer Presentation

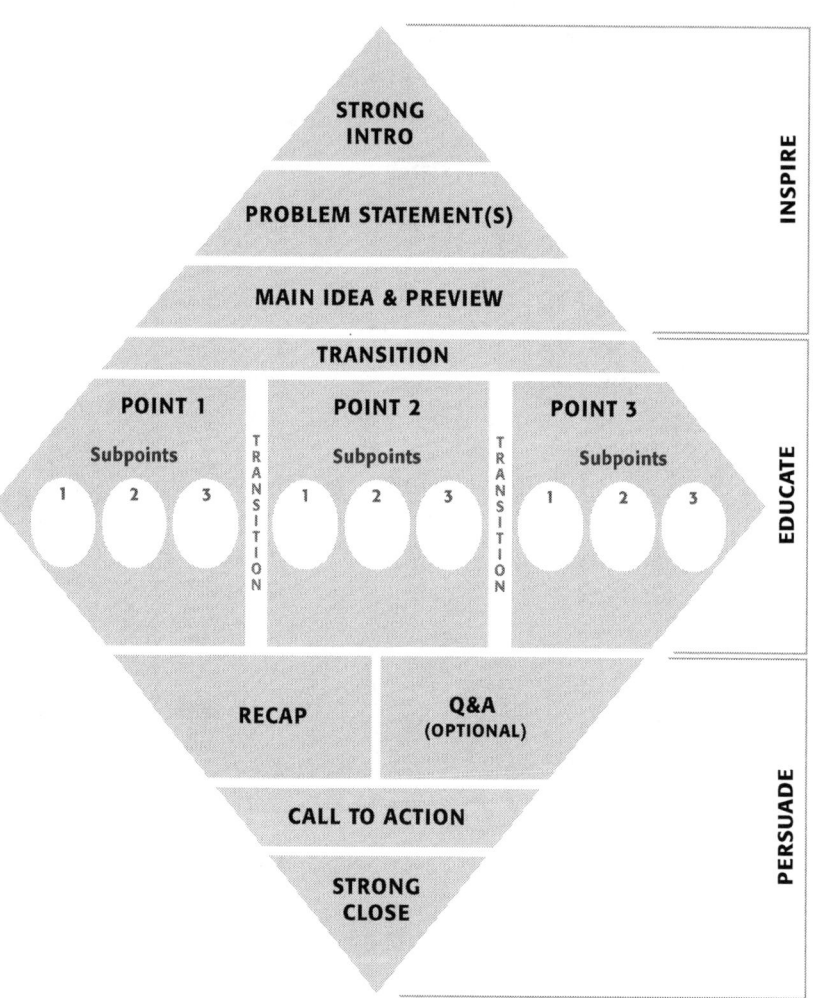

The Introduction establishes *why* the information is relevant to your audience, so as to create a connection with them. The goal is to *inspire* them to *feel* like the topic is valuable and beneficial to them.

The Body is where we establish *what* it is that we'll be talking about. Here is where the main concepts, facts, information, theories, stories, hypotheses, and proofs exist. This is the segment of the speech where we most want to *educate* our audience to *learn* from the expertise that we want to share with them.

The Conclusion is where we establish the *how*; how their lives will look if they do what you want them to do. This is the segment of the presentation where we want to *persuade* them to *do* something, and compel them to take action.

Start every presentation with the foundation of the Killer Presentation model, then move it into the Diamond. By doing so, you'll be crafting a presentation that is relevant, meaningful, and engaging to your audience – each and every time.

Common Questions About the Diamond

Q: **How long should each segment of the Diamond be in a speech?**

The Diamond is shaped in that way to reflect the relative length of each part of the speech.

The Strong Intro should be relatively short and immediately engaging. Your goal is to grab attention and set up interest in the rest of the speech fairly quickly. Then as you start moving through the Diamond, the elements gradually start to get longer. You would then need to spend more time setting up the Problem Statement, the essential message of your speech, and why this is important to the audience.

Moving further down the Diamond, you'll be spending a lot more time in the Body of the speech, discussing the Key Points and Sub-Points, including the facts, proofs, evidence, stories, examples, etc.

As you move into the speech's Conclusion, the segments of the Diamond start to get shorter again. The Recap quickly reviews the content, and the Call-to-Action directs the audience towards what they need to do next. The Q&A may take a little more time if your audience asks questions during this segment – or not, if your questions have already been asked throughout the speech or are waiting for the end. Then the Strong Close ends quickly, powerfully, and with impact, leaving your audience with a vision of what the future will be if they do what you suggest.

If we want to break this down even further, then we can say that if you have 30 minutes to present, that would amount to approximately 5 minutes for the Strong Intro, 20 minutes for the Body of the speech, and 5 minutes for the Strong Close.

Q: **Will too much structure and practice make me look over-rehearsed? Should I practice less, so that I can be more flexible with my content?**

You may wonder if preparing extensively is counterproductive. Does over-rehearsal make you present like a robot? Does it lock you into specific content, without any possibility for flexibility? Isn't it more powerful to "read" the audience and go from there?

In fact, a powerful structure actually allows you to be *more* creative, *more* flexible, and *more* confident in your speech.

Consider this: What if you get really nervous, your mind goes blank, and you forget what you want to say? Pretty terrifying, right? Adrenaline races through your body, you may be feeling increasing pressure as the audience watches and waits during the awkward silence, freaking out as you push your brain to the limit to think of something – *anything* – to say next, all amidst a heart beating so loudly that you can barely concentrate.

If – or when – a similar scenario has ever happened to you, how easy was it to find your way out of the situation?

 More structure, preparation and practice will provide you with even *more* flexibility in your presentations.

Chances are, it was not very easy. In fact, if you have ever experienced this personally, you probably found your way out of the predicament, but it likely would not have been very pleasant. Now consider how much *less* difficult it would be to have found your way out of that chaos if you had created a structured message and practiced your speech extensively.

Create the structure. Practice your presentation. Avoid the chaos.

Some of my clients who have experienced "blanking out" in front of their audiences were completely traumatized by it. They were embarrassed, felt like they failed, and thought they were judged harshly as a result. Some of them never wanted to give presentations again.

But eventually, they did give presentations again. Because the benefit of these kinds of awkward situations is that they are also amazing learning experiences. Most people are very motivated to do whatever it takes to make sure that these embarrassing situations never happen to them again.

When you're in front of your audience, it's up to you to deliver value and ensure that their time listening to you is well spent. With a strong structure, even if you have to veer off course during the speech to address the audience's questions, you can get yourself back on track.

If sudden inspiration hits and you decide to tell a story, share an experience, or introduce new content that you haven't previously practiced, you can still do so – and then get yourself back on track.

If you draw a blank and forget what you want to say, you can get yourself back on track.

Are you sensing a theme here?

The best part is, if your structure is strong, even your audience would be able to tell you where you left off. Now that's flexibility.

Common Mistakes When Using the Diamond

The Diamond provides guidance and offers flexibility to suit your presentation. However, that flexibility can lead to some common mistakes too.

1. **Too Many Points.** The Rule of Three consistently works well to guide you to keep the Key Points of your presentation focused and to the point. Yes, there are some exceptions to this rule, but choose these exceptions carefully. If you want to share 10

tips to managing stress, 12 ways to get in touch with your spiritual self, or 33 "must-dos" for organizing your office, write an article instead. Create a blog post. Give it away as a handout, along with all your contact information. Or choose 3 to 5 of your top ideas and go into greater detail on them. A long list of points is simply too much for an audience to take in, remember, and get value from. It induces audience fatigue. It's overwhelming. And the audience won't remember all of it. Covering too much information also means that you can't bring any one particular point to life, with examples, stories, and interaction.

2. **Winging It.** You may feel like you know your topic well enough, you'll remember what you need to say, and besides, you don't really have the time to put together the presentation anyway, so you'll just wing it. No problem, right?

   Big problem.

   Winging it does not allow for you to tailor your presentation to your audience properly. It assumes that you'll remember to say what you intend to say, and that you'll be able to make it relevant to the audience – which doesn't always happen when you're in an emotionally-charged state in front of a room of expectant (and sometimes judgmental) faces.

   When you put the time into preparing and even practicing your talk, not only are you respecting your audience by preparing something valuable for them in advance, but you're respecting yourself, and the knowledge that you want to share about that topic.

   And speaking of timing, the third mistake is …

3. **Going Over Time.** Please don't. I implore you. Audiences may love what you're saying, they may laugh at your stories, hang on the edge of their seats, participate and interact, but if you keep them longer than you promised, their opinion of you can turn very quickly. Many of us may have experienced that feeling of frustration when we're late for our next appointment because the speaker or meeting finished late. It's just a bad move, and one that can turn a very friendly audience into a very frustrated

one – one that does *not* leave with a good impression of the speaker. Respect your audience by sharing value, and then ending on time.

 Don't overload your audience with too much information. Avoid "winging it." And end your presentation on time. Ignoring any one of these pointers can turn a friendly, receptive audience into a frustrated one.

A Few Final Thoughts About the Diamond

- **Remember What Can Come from This.** When we get out in front of an audience, we owe it to them – and to ourselves – to be sure that our speech is compelling, engaging, and impactful. We may only have one shot in front of any particular audience. Having a strong, clearly structured speech, filled with information that is relevant, meaningful, and valuable is what will get you their attention, their connection, and the speaking results that you want.

- **Keep It Handy!** I've got a number of clients who tell me that they have the Diamond sitting on their desks, ready to be used as their "go-to roadmap" whenever a new presentation comes up. So why not keep it nearby for when you need to use it?

Now, Let's Make Your Diamond Shine Even Brighter!

There's one final piece of the Diamond that can make or break a presentation. One piece that contributes to building connection with your audience and creating an interesting, fun, and possibly even emotional journey. One piece that can back up your message, bring your facts to life, and really leave an impact.

Storytelling!

Done right, proper storytelling structure – whether you're telling a business story or a personal one – can elevate your presentation and create a message that is more impactful and memorable. This, in turn, gives *you* the ultimate bonus – namely, that you, and your message, become more memorable, more entertaining, and more impactful.

That is where we'll turn our attention in Chapter 5.

Seriously Skilled Storytelling: **The Shine**

> "PERSONAL STORIES ARE THE
> EMOTIONAL GLUE THAT
> CONNECTS YOUR AUDIENCE
> TO YOUR MESSAGE."
>
> ***Nancy Duarte***

Storytelling is an art form and has a place in every culture and society. Stories are a universal language that everyone – regardless of language, hometown, or heritage – can understand. They stimulate imagination and passion and create a sense of community among listeners and storytellers alike.

Stories can bring great value to a speech. They add interest and fun, they "give life" to facts and statistics, they show a concept in action, and, most importantly, they help you connect with, engage, and inspire an audience.

Alternatively, they can also be self-serving, drag on endlessly, and frustrate your audience. As a result, knowing which stories will deliver extraordinary meaning and value to your audience, and the proper way to tell them, is essential.

This chapter will address how to choose your most relevant stories for an audience, craft them using a specific storytelling structure, find useful ways to link your personal experiences into a business storytelling context, and how to use your story to relate to your audiences. In other words, this chapter will be transforming *you* into a skilled storyteller.

Making the Most of Your Personal Story

In Chapter 3, we talked about being clear on the objective of your presentation, and what you want your audience to learn, feel, or do as a result of hearing you speak. These objectives are the same when considering the storytelling aspect of your presentation.

Your stories must:

- Back up a key point – to *educate* your audience so that they *learn* something;

- Create a more emotional connection between the audience and your topic – essentially, to *inspire* your audience so that they *feel* something; and

- *Persuade* an audience to action – to compel them to *do* something.

Therefore, when you choose your stories, it is important to choose the ones that fit into these qualifications.

Five Essential Elements of Storytelling

According to HubSpot,[8] there are a few essential components that make for a great storytelling experience for both the reader and storyteller.

- **Entertaining:** Good stories keep the reader engaged and interested in what is coming next.
- **Educational:** Good stories spark curiosity and add to the reader's knowledge bank.
- **Universal:** Good stories are relatable for all readers and tap into emotions and experiences that most people have gone through.
- **Organized:** Good stories follow a structure that helps convey the core message and helps readers absorb it.
- **Memorable:** Whether through inspiration, drama, scandal, or humor, good stories stick in the reader's mind.

With that in mind, let's take a look at how to choose which of your stories and experiences fit into those elements and adapt them so that they resonate with your audiences.

The Good, the Bad, the Ugly ... and the Transformational

A common question that I hear is, "I don't really have any interesting stories about my life that are worth relating to an audience in a professional context. How do I work around that?"

Reflecting on your own personal experiences and determining whether they would be usable in a business context is a necessary first step. The truth is, you *do* have stories – but perhaps their importance simply hasn't been discovered yet. Take the time to reflect and ask yourself, "Which of my stories deliver genuine value, message, and expertise? Which ones help me pull my past together and into my present? Which ones get a little deeper to explain why I am who I am, and where I come from?"

There's no doubt that your story goes far deeper than "I grew up in this town, I went to school, travelled here, here and here, then this job, then this job, then I ended up where I am now." While that relates a chronological sequence of events, for it to qualify as an actual story, there are more targeted questions to ask. For example, where are the highs and the lows? Who are the "supporting characters?" Where's the conflict? Where are the learning points? What did you overcome – or not overcome?

 Your stories should reflect *transformational* moments in your life.

So where should you start? Look back at your life experiences. What are the funny stories, the good, the bad, and the ugly stories, the embarrassing stories, the silly stories, the stories of challenge, difficulty, mistakes, success, happiness, and learning experiences? Consider the interesting people you've met, the places you've traveled, important events from your past that have had a lasting impact on you, good advice that you've received, and the people who have made a difference in your life.

You're looking for the *transformational* moments, and the events that led up to them. These are the moments where something fundamentally changed, where you came to a new realization, you learned an important lesson, or things shifted in your world and your perspective. Being more aware of these experiences and how they made a difference to you can help your audience see how it might make a difference to them as well.

> *"Rather than telling people what you want them to do and hoping that they intellectually understand the instructions enough to do it – you can take them on a storytelling journey where they experience what you're saying for themselves."*
> DOUG STEVENSON

WHERE DO YOU FIND YOUR STORIES?

You don't have to have climbed Mount Everest, been in the Olympics, overcome a big trauma, or experienced a huge success to have a compelling story. If you need a little help on how to find some of your meaningful stories, try categorizing them into certain segments of your life. For example, consider stories and events having to do with your childhood, school, big events, relationships, life challenges, career, or travels. Tap into your past experiences and ask yourself these questions.

- Where do my life lessons come from?
- Did I ever experience a challenging or difficult event? How did I react at the time, and what was the learning from it?
- Who were the influencers/mentors in my life while I was growing up?
- How did I get to where I am in life, and what did I experience along the way that made a difference?
- What advice was I given that really impacted me?
- What mistakes have I made from which I was able to learn valuable lessons?

- Was there a time when I did something that really scared me, and how did it turn out?

For a list of questions designed to help draw out your stories, go to the exercise, Dig Out Your Stories, on pages 114–115.

You don't have to have climbed Mount Everest, been in the Olympics, overcome a big trauma, or experienced a huge success (or a huge failure) to have a compelling story. Sometimes small, even mundane events or moments can serve as the foundation to a captivating storytelling journey.

A FUNNY THING HAPPENED ON THE WAY TO FINDING MY STORY

Finding relevant stories does not always require you to delve deeply into your past. Maybe a relevant experience happened to you while picking up a coffee, having a conversation with a stranger, a routine trip to the bank, or showing up late to a meeting because of traffic or aliens landing in the middle of the highway. New and interesting stories may be happening to you every day. Stay aware of what's happening around you, what you learned from these experiences, and why it's relevant to you, your message, and your audience. Sometimes the smallest, most mundane events can make the most compelling stories of all.

Telling a story that doesn't have a point is a useless exercise. But a story with a point creates engagement, interest, and entertainment for the audience. And that makes both you – and your speech – much more memorable.

THE ROLE OF VULNERABILITY IN CREATING THE STORY

When people used to ask me, "How did you get into the public speaking field?" my standard answer used to go something like this.

"I started my company, Ideal Communications, in 2005, after witnessing the careers of educated, highly-intelligent people being hampered by their inability – or unwillingness – to speak in public. Through my training, workshops, and coaching, I started helping individuals create and deliver presentations with confidence and clarity."

A Word of Caution: Stories, Interests, Jokes, and Pop Culture References Aren't Universal

Early in my speaking career, I gave a public speaking workshop to a group of around 40 entrepreneurs. It was a group that had been meeting regularly for a few years, and I was already well-acquainted with many of the people in the room. It was a casual and fun atmosphere, so when I made a few risqué jokes to start the workshop, everyone got them, everyone laughed, and I considered it a success.

Three months later, I was invited to present a similar workshop to a different audience. This time, it was an audience that I didn't know, that didn't know me, and that didn't even know each other. Regardless, because of the great reactions in my last workshop, I decided to "warm up" the room by starting the workshop the same way, with the same risqué jokes.

Big mistake.

Not only did they not get it, but they didn't find it funny. It's also possible that a few people were offended by it. As soon as I said it, there was dead silence in the room.

You could hear a pin drop. A weird, awkward pin.

Given that I was expecting a similarly fun and laughter-filled response, the silence really threw me off my game. I did my best to move past this awkward moment and get back into my presentation's content as quickly as I could.

This painful lesson taught me not to start with a joke, or any off-color references, unless I totally know the audience and how they are likely to react. I didn't "read the room" at the beginning of the presentation and, as a result, I didn't know the audience well enough to pull off that kind of joke.

It's amazing how much a moment of embarrassment can teach you. For me, it was that what works for one audience will not necessarily work for another. Lesson learned.

 A story or joke that works for one audience will not necessarily work for another. You need to understand the audience – their needs, wants, their expectations, and even their sense of humor.

At the same time, over the years I've noticed other mistakes that have either alienated or disengaged an audience.

1. Sharing stories about people, topics, or places that the audience knows nothing about, without proper examples or a backstory to get everyone on the same page.

2. Using too many pop-culture references as part of the story. With today's international audiences, we can't assume that your audience knows as much as you do about certain topics, and it's not always possible to explain the premise to someone who isn't familiar with it. Not everyone is well-versed in Star Wars terminology, superhero trivia, breakfast cereals or classic movies from the 1980s.

Still, pop references can add a lot of levity and fun into a presentation and can highlight a point with impact. So what's the workaround? Feel free to include a pop culture reference or two, but don't structure your entire talk around it. Explain the meaning and context behind it so that the point can be understood, even if some of the people you're speaking to haven't watched that movie, heard that band, read that book, or seen that meme.

This "professional" answer would usually result in a blank stare or a fake smile, sometimes followed by an "Oh. Cool."

It didn't connect with people. It wasn't very interesting. And the fact is, it wasn't really true.

The full details of how I got into the public speaking field were shared in Chapter 2, but here's a recap.

When I was younger, I was very shy and quiet. Any sort of public speaking – whether in class, at work, or even in social settings – was something that I avoided at all costs. It made me feel uncomfortable, vulnerable, and, quite frankly, terrified. I was far happier as a wallflower and stayed far away from being the center of attention.

When I started my career as a professional speaker, I didn't want my audiences to know this truth. I thought that it was better for my credibility as a public speaker if I came across as an authority – and an extrovert – who had been destined for a life in front of an audience.

After all, I thought, "Who would want to work with a public speaking coach who used to *hate* public speaking?"

It was on the advice of a close colleague and friend who heard my real story and then pressed me with a frustrated-but-loving "Why aren't you sharing THAT story?!!?" question that compelled me to take a chance and dip my feet into revealing the truth.

The first time I shared the real story was in front of an audience of people I knew, who knew me, and who I trusted would be merciful if it turned out to be a failed experiment.

> *But what if the transformational moment makes you look like an amateur?*

What I did not expect was how my audience would better connect with my speech – and with me – by sharing my challenges, my insecurities, and learning how similar their story was to mine.

Somehow, my audience connected with my story and empathized with my earlier challenges because they could see themselves in it. It truly resonated with them and their past experiences. At the end of my presentation, there were more people than ever before coming up to me to share stories of how they grew up shy, how they avoided public speaking, and how they felt insecure about it.

The Five-Year-Old Who Built an Empire

One of my clients, an artist, entrepreneur, and creative business branding expert, was asked to give a presentation in front of a group of 100 business professionals. Not only did she want to make a good impression and create more visibility as an expert and a speaker, but she also wanted to make some sales to this audience of potential clients.

In our first session, which was intended for me to get to know her and her expertise a little better, she shared a story. When she was only five years old, she created handmade greeting cards and then sold them door to door in the apartment building where she lived to make a little extra money. As she told the story, she described how her mother watched over her and let her interact only with the people on her apartment floor. She knocked on doors, gave her sales pitch in her squeaky five-year-old voice, and sold the cards for 50 cents.

In the end, she sold a lot of them. As many of us already know, cute, industrious, and squeaky-voiced five-year-olds are adorably persuasive.

As she was very casually telling me this story, I could sense that she didn't fully grasp its relevance. But we very quickly set out to change that.

After a few minutes of discussion, she started to recognize how this story could both entertain and persuade her audience. Her strong tendencies towards art, entrepreneurship, and business from a very young age could easily be used as a meaningful selling point.

We took this story and developed it, scripted it, and polished it until it was one of her core signature stories.

Instead of *telling* the audience about her experiences selling her handmade cards, we *transported* them to the scene. We added imagery and visual details about what she wore, the pigtails in her hair, how she knocked on every door and delivered her sales pitch in her squeaky little five-year-old voice, and then how she asked for the sale. We also included the color of the apartment building's carpets, the length of the hallway, dialogue with her neighbors, and even described some of the bathrobe-wearing, cigarette-smoking, caught-by-surprise people who opened their doors to her for added visual imagery.

The more we could create these visual, auditory, and contextual details, the more entertaining it was for her audience. Our aim was for her audience to "see" all of these colorful details in their mind's eye. Maybe they'd even liken it to their own kids doing the same thing, or bring them back to their own experiences going door to door, selling chocolates or girl scout cookies, and reflecting on what they learned in that experience as well.

But most importantly, the point of her story was to show her audience, in a fun, engaging, and entertaining way, how she blended creativity and entrepreneurship from a very young age, and how she had been honing this skill for practically her entire life. With this kind of entrepreneurial background built into her DNA, her audience could more easily understand what she was capable of as a full-grown adult – and how her experience could help build *their* brands and businesses.

On top of all that, she had a blast telling this story.

Her audiences loved it. They connected with her because of it. And it was exactly what they needed to hear to understand how her long history as both an artist and an entrepreneur could help her art-centered clients build the businesses that they wanted.

This story, from a brief moment in time from her past, ended up having big meaning. Wrapped in an entertaining story, she used it at every subsequent speaking engagement to build her authority and credibility in the field, increase her reputation as a trusted leader, attract new clients, and build a little fun into her presentations.

They really connected with the story, and left feeling inspired that shyness, nerves, or general discomfort in public speaking didn't necessarily mean that they couldn't eventually become confident, impactful speakers.

It made a huge difference not only in the content of my presentations and how I delivered them, but, most importantly, it made me realize how swallowing my pride and allowing some vulnerability into my presentation made a huge difference in how I was able to connect with my audiences, and how they were able to connect with me. And that was the greatest result of all.

 Telling a story is like painting a picture with words.

Does Sharing My Stories Make a Presentation Too *Me-Focused*?

Here's a question that I often get asked about storytelling. "I want to tell my stories but I've been told that I shouldn't talk about myself in my presentations, but rather, that I should talk about the audience and their needs instead. Doesn't telling my stories make it more self-serving or *me-focused*, when what I really need to do is to make it *you-focused*, focused on the audience?"

A valid question.

There's no public speaking rule that says that you can never talk about yourself in your presentations. You've lived your own life up to now, and your experiences have created who you are and what you know. The key is to know what kind of stories the audience will relate to, which ones will turn them off, and why you're sharing these particular stories at all.

As mentioned earlier in this chapter, the best stories about you are the ones that share a transformational moment, where you came to a new realization, where things shifted in your world, your perspective, or your experience. These types of stories may reflect a challenge that you faced or uncomfortable moments in your life, and

But if I talk about me, then I'm not talking about them. Isn't that a problem?

what you learned from them. Those are far more powerful than if you simply gave them a laundry list of successes.

But here's the most critical element in your stories. Your audience needs to be able to relate to them. The more your story can be seen, experienced and translated into each audience member's experience, the more meaning and value they will derive from it.

Still not sure how to pinpoint the stories from your past that may qualify as transformational moments? Here are several questions that will help you identify some core events from your life that can be added to your presentations to add interest, meaning, and audience engagement.

Even those brief moments in time from your past, which you may think are fairly inconsequential, can have a powerful message behind them. Be open to the thoughts that might pop up while you do this exercise.

PERSONAL REFLECTIONS

Childhood Experiences

1. As a child, what did you want to be when you grew up?
2. What experiences stand out from your childhood?
3. What games did you enjoy playing?
4. Growing up, did you ever feel "different" from the rest of the crowd? If so, in what way?

Life Lessons

5. Who were the influencers/mentors in your life while you were growing up? Parents? Grandparents? Other relatives? Teachers? Coaches? How did they impact you?
6. What advice did they give you that you did or did not act on?
7. Who are your mentors now?
8. What mistakes have you made in the past that you were able to learn something from?
9. Was there a time when you did something that really scared you? What was it? What was the outcome, and the learning?
10. Was there a time when you did something really dumb? What was it? What was the outcome, and the learning?

GENERAL QUESTIONS

11. What is your favorite movie? Why?
12. What is your favorite fiction or non-fiction book? Why?

13. Did you have any hobbies growing up? What were they?

14. Did you play any sports or were you involved in an organized physical activity (i.e., dance, gymnastics, martial arts) as a child/teen/adult?

15. Do you have any special talents that not many people know about (i.e., magic, juggling, chef, reiki master, play a musical instrument, etc.)?

16. Think back to all the trips/travel you've taken. Are there any that stand out because of something extraordinary (good or bad)?

17. What bothers you?

18. What adversities have you overcome in your personal life?

19. Who are your most interesting friends/family members?

20. What advice would you give your 10-year-old-self now? (This is one of my favorites!)

21. What do you know *now* that a few years ago you could not imagine knowing?

22. What are you most proud of in your life?

PROFESSIONAL REFLECTIONS

23. List the jobs that you had over the course of your career.

24. Which ones were the best? Why?

25. Which ones were the worst? Why?

26. Were there any bosses/coworkers who made a real difference in your life (i.e., taught you something that you use even today)?

27. What was the chain of events that led you onto your current career path? In other words, how did you end up in the career you're in right now?

28. What adversities have you overcome in your professional life?

29. If you could go back in time and change the course of your career, what would you do differently?

30. What other stories are you reminded of – right now – after answering all these questions?

Business Storytelling: Making Your Product, Service, or Customer Experiences Come Alive

While everyone can tell a story, some people are able to fine-tune their storytelling skills and become a storyteller on behalf of their organization, brand, or business. Sharing your business or client stories will show how your solution has helped others, in a way that resonates with the needs and emotions of your audience. This job may fall on the marketers, the copywriters, or the public relations department of your organizations. Or it may fall directly on *your* shoulders.

Regardless of where it lands, there are many reasons we should look towards business storytelling as one of the key elements to helping us connect with our prospects, clients, and audiences.

- **Stories Solidify Abstract Concepts and Simplify Complex Messages.** Trying to understand a new idea can sometimes be confusing, and stories can help by simplifying abstract concepts and complex messages. For example, think about times when stories have helped you better understand a concept: maybe a professor explained a science problem using a real-life example, a parent taught their child a new skill by sharing how they approached it at their age, or a salesperson used a case study to convey how they solved a client's problem instead of relying on complex data or technical jargon that very few customers would understand.

 Facts and figures and all the "rational" information that we think is important in the business world don't stick in our minds as much as we may think they do (or should). But by attaching emotions to situations, we can create more memorable stories.

- **Stories Can Educate, Inspire, and Persuade – And Answer *"Why?"*** On both a personal and corporate level, stories create a level of vulnerability, transparency, and authenticity. They uncover not just *what* you're selling, but *why* you're selling it, often in a creative and engaging way. This creates an emotional bond that allows prospects, clients, and consumers to connect with you, which then helps you market your product or service, build loyalty, and drive action.

TAKING YOUR SALES PITCH TO THE NEXT LEVEL

When you're in front of a prospect or client, your best sales pitch is to share the stories of your clients' successes in a way that showcases what you (or your organization) did for them. When you share stories of how your solution has helped others who had a similar problem, you can actually sing your praises and talk about how valuable your solution is – without looking like you're actually bragging. Your strategically chosen stories can help to overcome resistance and answer questions faster and more effectively than is possible with features, benefits, and data.

Think of it this way: your competitor's products may be high quality, with great features and benefits. They may even be cheaper. If that's the case, why would a client choose you over your competition?

Because they trust you. They believe that they will have a good relationship with you. And they connect with you on a more emotional level.

All this is achieved with seriously skilled storytelling structure.

 Business storytelling overcomes resistance and answers questions faster and more effectively than features, benefits, and data.

The Five-Step Business Storytelling Structure

Use this five-step business storytelling structure to help you identify and build the framework of your business stories. (Your Business Storytelling Roadmap, an exercise that appears on page 119, will give you the opportunity to apply these five steps.)

1. **Who:** Who was the protagonist or main character of the story? (*Hint:* It's usually the client you helped.)
2. **Problem:** What was the problem that they were experiencing? How were they affected by it, from both a personal and

organizational perspective? How was it affecting their growth, creating frustration, or causing them to lose money? (*Hint:* It was bad ... oh so bad ... and, coincidentally, so similar to what the person or organization you may *currently* be speaking with is experiencing.)

3. **Solution:** What was the solution? (*Hint:* This is where you come in.)

4. **Execution:** How was the solution implemented? (*Hint:* How did you support them during this implementation?)

5. **Results:** Where are they now? (*Hint:* Probably in a much better place, now that their problem has been solved – thanks to you!)

Ensure that your audience can relate to your story by:

- Targeting it to the person (or group) to whom you will be speaking, and

- Choosing examples of clients/industries that are similar to the ones to whom you are presenting.

Doing this will help you create a story that is far more meaningful and relevant for your audience, with the ultimate goal of building higher levels of connection, trust, and better business results.

MERGING PERSONAL AND PROFESSIONAL STORIES

You don't necessarily need to shy away from telling personal stories in a professional context. Consider your own life experiences for ways to illustrate your message and showcase the idea you are trying to share. This may include:

- Past mistakes that ultimately led to success;

- Lessons learned through experience; or

- Struggles, failures, and challenges that have been overcome.

The willingness to show vulnerability in the stories that you share will make you look more authentic and is more likely to create a deeper level of trust and emotional connection with your audience.

The ultimate goal of business storytelling is to create an emotional connection that shows why you are the right choice for the client; that you understand your client's needs, challenges and goals; and that you have the right experience, resources, and solutions to help them achieve the results that they desire.

COACHING EXERCISE *Your Business Storytelling Roadmap*

Use this five-step storytelling framework to help you formulate your stories and share past experiences, including how you have helped past clients. You will create a deeper level of trust, connection, and interest with your prospect, client, or audience.

1. **WHO:** Who is the main character?

   _____

   _____

2. **PROBLEM:** What was the problem? How were they affected by it?

   _____

   _____

3. **SOLUTION:** What was the solution?

   _____

   _____

4. **EXECUTION:** How was the solution implemented?

   _____

   _____

5. **RESULTS:** Where are they now?

   _____

   _____

Lead, inspire, and engage your audience through compelling storytelling!

The Wealthy Entrepreneur Whose Success Story Bored Everyone to Tears

I once attended a meeting to hear a talk by a well-known business figure who was invited to speak to a group of female entrepreneurs to share his success story. Many people spoke highly of him, and I was interested to hear what he had to say and how learning from his experiences might help me build my business.

When this man started speaking, he was very engaging, full-of-life, and charismatic. His stories were fun and interesting to listen to, and he told them with excitement and energy. As I looked around the room, I could tell that everyone was paying attention, eager to learn from him, and really enjoying what he was saying.

But after several minutes, the audience started fading. His stories, while told with the same intensity, smile, and enthusiasm, just didn't hit the mark anymore. The energy in the room was like a balloon with the air slowly being let out.

As I looked around the room at the not-quite-as-amused-anymore faces, I wondered, "What went wrong?"

I mean, super-successful dude had an authentic, engaging energy about him. That was a definite plus.

His stories were quite interesting. Another plus.

He was passionate about the work he did. Awesome.

But a presentation filled with interesting stories needs to be sustained not only by energy and interesting content, but by content that's *relevant to the audience.*

Here's what went wrong.

1. **They Couldn't Relate.** His audience was full of entrepreneurs, all women, many of whom were balancing their businesses, their families, their friends, their homes, their health and well-being, and other demands on their time. They were not, in all likelihood, always able to bring their business to its fullest potential because of these many demands, despite the passion and love for what they did. As a result, when he told stories about leaving his family to live in another city for

a year, hopping on a plane to Asia with three-hours' notice, and being able to jump on every single opportunity thrown at him – no matter what time of day, and no matter wherever in the world it was – because his wife supported him by being able to take care of the home, kids, and life while he ran around the globe chasing business, it just wasn't relatable. Most women in the audience simply couldn't connect with the "drop everything and go" stories. It wasn't a life that they could lead and, for most of them, nor was it even one that they wanted to. And once they couldn't relate, it was a slippery slope to disengagement and disconnection.

2. **The I/You Ratio.** There was a lot of "I" did this, "I" went here, "I" worked there. Not a lot of "you" references until the very end, when he left us with his "three pieces of advice that I learned along the way that you can leave with." This advice was actually quite valuable, but it only came *all* the way at the end of the presentation. Perhaps had he woven those pieces of advice throughout the presentation, his audience might have stayed more attentive.

3. **He Was the Hero of All the Stories.** Just about every decision he made turned out well. Great people came his way. Great opportunities came his way. Then even *better* opportunities came his way. The more he talked about how great his life was, the more the audience shut down. Stories about success on top of success are much less engaging than those that share struggles or challenges faced along the way. What mistakes could he have shared that we all could have learned from? Where were the juicy details of difficulties that he faced, challenges that he overcame, or things that didn't go as planned?

Ultimately, super-successful dude was invited to speak to "tell his story." And we wanted to hear his story. We wanted to hear how he got to where he was in life. His was a real success story, and he had a lot of knowledge and experience to share with those who hadn't yet attained his level of success.

But because those of us in the audience couldn't relate to his experiences, it just didn't work. We knew it, and with the dwindling energy of the group, he knew it too.

 Choose your stories carefully. Don't be the hero of all your stories, where everything that happened to you worked out exactly as you planned or only led to success. Audiences won't connect with that.

Same Story; Different Approach

Let's take super-successful dude from the Speaker Story above. He was asked to present at this meeting to share his stories, and he was proud to share them because, after all, they *were* his stories, and they reflected how he got to where he was in life. But what could he have done differently, using those same stories, to enhance connection with the audience?

What if, halfway through the speech, he had added in a qualifying statement, something like this: "I know that many of you in the audience aren't necessarily positioned to follow a career path like I had. I was lucky to have my wife and kids support me when I had to live in another city, and they accepted that I wouldn't be there for many holidays and weekends. I was lucky to be able to hop on a plane at a moment's notice, and to be given so many opportunities. Many of you might not be in that same position, and I get that. But whatever your current situation, or however much you're balancing all the aspects of your life, there are certain things that I've learned along the way that were critical to growing my business and attracting opportunities, regardless of whatever else might have been pulling at my attention at the time. So, I'll share the top three things I learned along the way that you can use to grow your business, no matter where you're at or what other priorities you're balancing in your life."

Had he just acknowledged that fact, it could have been a highly effective way to relate to the audience and acknowledge our life situations, challenges, and motivations. I believe that this, in turn, would have made all of us far more attentive to his stories, and the lessons that could have been learned from them.

You can stay true to your story as long as you stay true to delivering value and relevance for your audience.

How a Story of Past Failure Turned into a Giant Success

Andrea was a high-ranking sales executive at a pharmaceutical company when she was asked to give a presentation at the annual company conference. Despite having been at the company for only five months, in this presentation she would have to address the fact that her team of 150+ people hadn't met their sales targets, and, as a result of that, they weren't going to get their bonuses. On top of that, she had to create a positive spin to this message and persuade her just-about-to-hear-that-they're-not-getting-a-bonus team to adopt and follow a new sales strategy for the next year.

And if all that wasn't difficult enough — and let's be clear, it *was* difficult enough — given that she was still fairly new at the company, Andrea hadn't personally met all the members of her team yet and hadn't had the time to fully connect with them or establish her leadership position in the group. She did know, however, that as a high-ranking executive in the organization, many of the junior managers were inspired by her, considered her a role model, and looked up to her.

It was essential for her to find a way to connect with the audience and build trust, so that she could influence the team's future behavior.

She knew that she could educate them in a meaningful way about the details of the new sales strategy and why following it would help them reach their sales numbers, which was important not only to the future of the company but to their own professional future as well.

To her, that was the easy part.

She also knew that she had to persuade them to take action. She was less worried about this part because the new sales strategy she was introducing had a very clear execution approach. She was confident that the team would know what actions they would have to take to move forward once this strategy was put in place.

By the time she came to me, Andrea needed guidance in figuring out what she needed to say to *inspire* the team so that they could see the *value* of changing the old sales strategy and adopting the new one. They had to understand how much more effective it would be towards supporting their efforts and reaching their sales goals. She knew that she had to trigger the emotions and the feelings that would make them *want* to push forward and adopt it.

We decided that Andrea would share the story of a past experience 12 years earlier, when she was in a sales position similar to those in the audience. She told the story about a terrible day filled with rejections, missed appointments, rude people, smoking endless cigarettes, spilled coffee, a flat tire, pouring rain, and sitting in her car … crying. It was a complete failure of a day.

She didn't just tell the story, she showed it. She recounted dialogue and conversations she had. She created visuals about sitting in her blue Ford Escort, running in the rain with a broken umbrella, spilling coffee on her favorite white top. She moved around the stage performing the actions – and the emotions – she experienced on that day. She let the audience see, and feel, exactly what she went through. It was the good, the bad, and the ugly – but mostly the bad and the ugly.

And the audience was riveted.

How could it be that such a high-level executive, in charge of so many people at this company, would allow herself to be vulnerable enough to show such a moment of weakness?

It could be – and it was – incredibly effective.

She followed up this dramatic, performance-based story by sharing how she seriously considered quitting her job at her lowest, most emotional point. But the next morning, she woke up filled with renewed determination and decided instead to throw herself back into her work. She shared the exact steps that she took to shift her mindset, tame her frustration, and get her sales calls back on track.

She shared the changes that she made, not only to *how* she worked, but how she *thought about* her work, and the impact that those changes had on her success ever since.

Her ultimate focus was on the challenges that she experienced, the lessons learned, and how those lessons could be made meaningful to the audience in front of her on that day.

How did it all go?

She brought the house down. Her audience absolutely *loved* the story. Poking fun at her vulnerable moment allowed her to create a powerful emotional connection with her team. Not only did it inspire them, but it made them more willing to buy into her vision of the new strategic sales plan. It also shifted them away from the negative context that they started with, when they were informed that they wouldn't be getting their bonuses.

This particular story – just a small moment in her life, so many years earlier – set her up as not just their boss, but someone who had been where they are, and truly understood their challenges. Her authenticity was off the scale.

In addition to that, the story highlighted the exact behaviors that she wanted and needed from her team, by sharing how she went after and accomplished her tasks and goals.

And while she was the central figure in the story, she didn't make herself the hero. Rather, by the end of the talk, when she was rallying the team to adopt the new strategy and building a Visionary Conclusion around the successes that she was sure *they* would be celebrating a year in the future, she made the *audience* into the hero.

It was a game-changer.

At the end of her story, she very honestly told her team that the road ahead was going to be tough, but if they all pulled together, they would accomplish everything they needed to in the end. But by this point in her presentation, she didn't have to demand change or effort. Everyone was so emotionally invested with her and her story by then, and she had built such a high level of trust and connection, that they wanted to be part of the journey.

In the week following Andrea's presentation, she was approached by members of her team, her colleagues, and company executives to discuss her presentation. They congratulated her, they thanked her, they told her how brave they thought she was for sharing her story. Most importantly, they shared how they had gone through similar moments of weakness and frustration, and how meaningful it was for them to know that she had as well, because it showed that she really understood them and their challenges.

To say that she made an impact on everyone in that room is an understatement.

The bottom line? Andrea's success in that presentation came from a life experience that was re-created in a business storytelling context to build connection, motivate hundreds of people, and inspire change.

Stories like Andrea's happen in our lives all the time.

Small moments in time can end up being meaningful to you, your life lessons, and your audience. Start becoming more aware of them. Write them down. They happen for a reason. And that reason may be because eventually they can be used to inspire others.

Build Your Brand, Business, and Credibility with Your Stories

Use client stories to share examples of how amazing you are!

The fact is, those who can create and tell compelling stories have a powerful advantage over others.

And fortunately, anyone can become a better storyteller.

What's Next?

Now that you've completed this chapter, you have the tools to:

- Understand the value of your expertise, and why it should be shared with others;
- Manage your speaking nerves and build your confidence before stepping out in front of a group;
- Build Killer Presentations that educate, inspire, and persuade your audience;
- Use the Diamond to create structured, engaging, and powerful presentations; and

- Add compelling stories that bring color, inspiration, and an emotional connection to your speech.

Now it's time to put it all together and to deliver it with confidence, style, and personality.

Let's move on to Chapter 6 and make it happen!

Putting It All Together: Let's Do This!

> "TAKE ADVANTAGE OF EVERY
> OPPORTUNITY TO PRACTICE YOUR
> COMMUNICATION SKILLS, SO THAT
> WHEN IMPORTANT OCCASIONS
> ARISE, YOU WILL HAVE THE GIFT,
> THE STYLE, THE SHARPNESS, THE
> CLARITY, AND THE EMOTIONS
> TO AFFECT OTHER PEOPLE."
>
> *Jim Rohn*

Take a deep breath, take a look at what you've accomplished so far, and pat yourself on the back for doing the work.

You've committed to speak up, share your voice, and create value for your audience.

You've taken steps to manage your nerves and build your confidence.

You've learned how to apply useful tools to understand your audience so that you can customize your presentation in a way that educates, inspires, and persuades them. You can now create a message that's valuable to them and far more likely to get the results that you want.

You've gone through the Diamond, researched every piece, lovingly and thoughtfully structured your presentation, and crafted it in a way that is meaningful and relevant to the audience.

You've shaped your professional and personal stories to make them entertaining and impactful, to create a connection with your audience, and to deliver a much more engaging experience.

And Now, It's Go Time!

The time has come for you to raise your hand and speak up, prepare to get up in front of the room, on the stage, or in that virtual meeting, and deliver your presentation to a live audience!

In previous chapters, our focus was on creating *what* you want to say. In this chapter, we'll be talking about *how* you say it.

How can you ensure that all those carefully chosen words in your presentation actually come out of your mouth the way you intended?

How can you get a better idea of what the audience is seeing when they watch and listen to you, so that you can do more of what works, and less of what doesn't?

How can you know if your body language is natural, your voice is strong, your pause is purposeful, and your slides are engaging?

And how can you be sure that the true, authentic you shows up when you're in front of that group of people – or that one important person – listening to your message?

Read on, and you'll find out.

Your Game-Day Attitude

 To ensure a successful presentation, you've got to manage your anticipation, your nerves, and your mindset.

By now you've probably realized that it takes a fair amount of work to craft and deliver a structured, engaging, compelling presentation, which often includes the following:

- Deciding what information goes into your presentation;
- Researching the facts and information;
- Creating the talking points and assessing the focus and flow;

- Coming up with relevant examples;
- Designing the slides;
- Practicing;
- Choosing what you're going to wear; and
- Getting in front of your audience – an audience of one or many – and delivering it.

But as the big day arrives, how can you manage your mindset and handle the anticipation (or anxiety) that lies ahead?

THE "GO GET 'EM!" SPEAKER

This is the speaker who is excited to give their presentation, pumping themselves up beforehand with affirmations, visualizations, and maybe even power posing and jumping jacks (as long as they're not in heels). Bouncing all the way to the stage, they're assured that they're going to nail it!

According to Forbes, that type of speaker comprises about 10% of the population.[9]

Then there's the rest of us.

Are you more the "Go get 'em!" or the "They're out to get me!" speaker?

THE "THEY'RE OUT TO GET ME!" SPEAKER

Most of us fall into this category, showing that it is natural to have some apprehension as the big day gets closer. This type of speaker may have some (or all) of the following thoughts going through their minds in the moments before they speak, and maybe even as they start their presentation.

- "I'm so nervous."
- "My voice is shaking."
- "How should I stand?"
- "How should I move?"
- "What should I do with my arms?"
- "Is my voice clear enough?"
- "Am I energetic enough?"

- "Am I saying 'um' too much?"
- "My hands are so sweaty."
- "My mouth is really dry."
- "My face must be getting so red."
- "They can probably tell how nervous I am."
- "Why aren't they laughing – they're supposed to laugh!"
- "Are they getting this?"
- "Someone just yawned. Are they bored?"
- "Do they even care what I'm talking about?"
- "What if I forget what I want to say?"
- "Is that guy looking at his phone instead of watching me?"
- "It's so hot in here."
- "Maybe if I speak faster it'll be over sooner."
- "Why did I even agree to this?"

Deep breath!
Why is all this even happening?

Because public speaking is risky. It takes time, effort and focus to create a valuable experience for an audience, and to make yourself look like a trusted leader – and, yes, maybe even a speaking superstar – in the process.

The good news is, your speech delivery is highly influenced by your speech structure. And if you've been following this book and applying everything that you've learned so far about speech structure … that bodes well for your public speaking future!

Structure – For Confidence and Speech Delivery

As we covered in Chapter 4, a strong speech structure is critical to helping you deliver your presentation with confidence, clarity, and control. Simply put, if you want to manage your nerves before a presentation, you need to spend the time structuring it properly.

Why is this so necessary? Let's recap.

When your presentation is based on a strong structure – which gets you clear on the message, clear on your audience and their struggles, clear on your Key Points, your stories, your Calls-to-Action, and clear on the value that it and you provide – your presentation becomes something that you *want* to share. The excitement of delivering a focused, engaging, structured speech that has you, and your unique personality woven into it, becomes much more powerful than the nerves.

Now that you know that strong, structured content will help you deliver with more confidence, let's look at the other elements that can help – and sometimes hinder – your speaking success once you're in front of your audience.

The Power – Or the Peril – Of Your Slides

PowerPoint, Keynote, Google Slides, Prezi, Zoom virtual backgrounds, or whatever other slide technology is yet to come can be used to engage the audience and highlight your message in a visual, stimulating way. It can also be a tool that bores the audience and distracts them from the real stars of the show – which are you and your message!

Not everyone in your audience can read and listen at the same time.[10] As soon as you put up a text-heavy slide or a slide with lots of text and images floating around, their eyes move away from you and over to the slides. This breaks the connection with you and can distract your audience.

Do your slides support your points or put everyone to sleep?

Slides are only meant to be a visual aid. *You* and *your content* should be the primary focus. In other words, you don't want to compete with *yourself* for the audience's attention.

 Slides are a visual aid only. *You* and *your content* are the stars of the presentation.

YOUR SLIDE GUIDE

Here are a few guidelines to keep in mind when it comes to slide content and slide delivery that will ensure they support you in creating and delivering an impactful presentation.

1. **Build Your Structure, *Then* Your Slides.** So many people "throw together" a bunch of slides when it's time to prepare a presentation, and it becomes more of an information dump than a proper slide presentation. But if you've learned anything in this book, it's that structure is the most important element to a speech. Get clear on your message, and only *after* you've set up your structure and outline does it make sense to build the slides.

2. **Add Images for Visual Impact.** An image can tell a story, share a message, or add a visual cue that enhances a presentation. Additionally, given that 65% of the population are visual learners,[11] adding images to your slides will certainly help drive your point home. This is your chance to be creative and choose a visual that backs up your story in a fun, insightful, or surprising way. And even if you're not very creative, the many image sites available online can make your search much easier. Just put in a few key words, and you will get plenty of options to help you flex your creative muscle. Just be sure to describe the images in your presentations, so that any members of your audience who are visually impaired don't have to feel left out of any of your great content.

    A word of caution, however. Certain animations can trigger nausea, headaches, and dizziness in people with inner ear disorders. Additionally, if the image content strobes or flashes rapidly, it may trigger seizures in people with photosensitive epilepsy. This is important to keep in mind, especially when showing videos or animated gifs.[12]

A picture is worth (a thousand) spoken words! Adding images, graphics, and drawings can help bring a concept to life – and it's very useful for visual learners!

3. **Be Careful with Colors.** Since your audience must always be able to see your text clearly, keep the text and background color scheme simple. Black text on a white background, or white text on a black background is best. You can also have darker colored

text on a white background. But once you start messing around with the colors of the rainbow as text or background, you risk your audience straining their eyes – or not being able to see the content of your slides altogether. Given that color blindness affects 1 of every 12 men (8%), and 1 of every 200 women (0.5%), keeping the colors simple to view ensures that your presentation is more visually accessible to everyone.[13] If, however, color is an important part of your presentation, then enhance them with labels, graphics, and icons. The bottom line is, don't rely only on colors to tell your story.

4. **Keep Text to a Minimum.** Take out any unnecessary words. Keep it clean, clear, and quick to read. The text on your slides can be used as reminders of what you need to say next, but they are there for the benefit of the audience.

5. **Go Big or Go Home.** Ensure that the font size is large enough for your audience to read from everywhere in the room – or on their computer screens. If delivering an in-person presentation, be mindful that people at the back of the room, and those with vision impairments, will appreciate the larger text as well.

6. **Charts? Graphs?** The downside of using charts and graphs can be that the font size of the explaining text is sometimes very small. In cases like this, it's more effective to highlight a particular piece of the chart or graph, enlarge the font of that specific text, circle it, or point an arrow to it. Make it easy for your audience to see what you want to show them.

7. **Don't Read Your Slides.** That's it. Just don't do it. You're there to speak to your audience, not to read your slides.

8. **Know When to Turn Off Your Slides.** When you're telling a story or wish to shift audience attention to you instead of your slide, press "B" on your keyboard. Most wireless presenters (in highly technical terms, also known as "the clicker") will have this feature as well. This will make your slide go black, thereby shifting your audience's attention 100% back to you. Then hit that very same key to bring the slides back into view when you're ready to return to your slides.

9. **Prepare for Technology Failures and Have a Backup Plan Ready.** Always be ready to present without your slides in case you experience a technology failure. It can happen, and if you've ever experienced it personally you can probably attest to how upsetting it is. If your technology doesn't work as you need it to, you may have to make a very quick decision as to whether you're better off:

   - Continuing to fiddle around with your setup hoping to fix it;
   - Keeping your audience waiting for you; or
   - Moving forward with your presentation, without the slides. (For the record, most audiences will choose this option!)

10. **Do You Actually *Know* Your Content?** In some organizations, one individual may be tasked to present updates from his team to management. This often means that multiple team members will put together slides related to the tasks that they're working on and will combine it all into one presentation, which is then delivered by one individual. This presenter may then deliver the information given to them without having the appropriate context to know what it means. In these situations, there's a big risk that the presenter may be asked a question about content on their slides, and they won't know the answer. While there are certainly ways to say "I don't know" in a professional, credible manner (see page 91), you typically don't want to share information if you don't understand it fully. As the speaker, you're expected to know the material on your slides, so take the time to better understand what you're presenting. And if it's too complex, you can always ask the person who provided you with that information to deliver that portion of the slides. That way, you give *them* the visibility, and you keep *your* credibility high.

Body Language, Gestures, Movement, and Posture

Consider all the time and effort spent putting together the right content for your presentation ... and then you get in front of your audience and fidget, move, and pace without purpose. This will ultimately distract your audience, but often, it can distract you as well. And that's a problem.

Before I go on to share with you what body language techniques you *need* to implement in order to nail your next presentation and have your audience hanging on your every word, let me just say one thing.

There are actually *no* body language techniques that you need to implement in order to nail your presentation and have your audience hanging on your every word!

Seriously.

This is both good news *and* bad news. But it's mostly good news.

 When it comes to gestures and body language, it's important that you move in a way that feels natural and authentic to you.

To be clear, there are always guidelines as to what you should try to avoid when speaking in front of a group, or to that one important person in front of you. It helps to be aware of movements and gestures that can distract – or even turn off – your audience, such as:

- Finger-pointing;
- Speaking in monotone;
- Avoiding eye contact;
- Slouching or other forms of bad posture; and
- Fidgeting and other distracting movements, such as:
  - Swaying from side to side;
  - Flipping your hair;
  - Playing with your rings;
  - Grasping your fingers;
  - Touching the change or keys in your pocket;
  - Hooking your fingers into your belt loops;
  - Putting your hands in your back pockets;
  - Leaning back on your heels;
  - Crossing your legs, one in front of the other … and then back again; and
  - Moving or pacing aimlessly on a stage or in front of a room.

THE ONE THING YOU SHOULD DO IS JUST BE YOU

There is the only rule you *must* follow when speaking, and that is: move, gesture, and speak in a way that feels comfortable for *you*!

There are speakers who keep moving around a stage and don't stop – like Tony Robbins. There are some who stand in one spot, and don't move at all – like Sir Ken Robinson. Some stand behind a podium and share lots of stories – like Jane Goodall. There are those who move around – consciously, unconsciously, and with or without purpose – like Sheryl Sandberg or Jamie Oliver. And some whose every move is scripted and deliberate – like Steve Jobs was known to do.[14]

> *"Be yourself, because everyone*
> *else is already taken."*
>
> OSCAR WILDE

The point is, every single speaker has their own unique speaking style, and it is this authenticity that will help an audience connect with you and your message. As soon as you try to copy someone else's style, it shows. Invest your time in getting comfortable with what feels right for you when you're in front of that key audience, so that you can always be the best version of yourself.

WHO IS THAT SPEAKER? OH, WAIT, IT'S ME!

A few years ago, I was presenting brand-new content that I had created specifically for a group of around 100 product managers. I had written and re-written the messages countless times. I included examples, stories, videos, and interactive work. I moved on and off the stage, walked around the room, made jokes, had fun slides, and pulled out whatever I could from my speaker's toolbox to engage this audience.

I gave that speech, and that audience, every ounce of energy that I had. I even hired a videographer to record the presentation so that I could learn from it, and, if it was good enough, use it in my marketing.

The *other* new thing that I was attempting on that day was to slightly alter my speaking style – change it just a *little* bit – to emulate another speaker who inspired me, and whose style I absolutely loved. This was someone who commanded a room, and who could some-times be intensely serious, and at other times be very funny; someone whose delivery was precise and yet who could improvise at a moment's notice; someone who exuded confidence and energy, who had the audience hanging on her every word; and someone who truly embodied what I knew a powerful speaker to be.

Overall, my presentation went well enough. The feedback was good. My colleague who attended said that it was very engaging. A few attendees came up to me afterwards and said that the content was very relevant to them. The person who hired me was satisfied.

A few weeks later, my video editor sent me the recording. I couldn't wait to see it.

And when I watched it, I couldn't believe what I saw.

My first thought was, "Who the heck is *that?*"

I was so serious – overly serious. I didn't smile nearly as much as I thought I did. There were points where I felt like I was almost reprimanding my audience. "Do this" and "don't do that" and "you won't get the results you want" and other doom and gloom.

Even though I felt like I put a ton of energy into the speech that night, it didn't seem to show up on video.

It didn't even look like I was having any fun!

Compared to how I *thought* I looked to that audience and in other videos of past presentations, I barely recognized myself.

I didn't like what I saw on the video. And I was so upset.

At first, I asked myself *how* this could have happened? How could there be such a disconnect between how I felt during the presentation, and what came across on the video?

After much reflection, I considered that one possible reason that my speaking style was so "off" may have been a direct result of being nervous about delivering brand-new content. I was nervous about forgetting key points, telling a story in a way other than I had intended, that the audience wouldn't laugh where they were supposed to, or that they might not "get it." Fair enough.

But when I dug a little deeper, I realized that the other reason that I couldn't recognize myself was because I was trying to deliver my talk like someone else. I was trying to speak like her, move like her, emote like her.

Except I'm not her.

Which is why I couldn't pull it off.

And the camera caught that.

Thankfully, neither the audience nor the person who hired me caught it, because they were only able to judge the presentation that I delivered. They don't know what I could (or *should*) have been.

That day, I learned that it's perfectly OK to be inspired by and learn from someone's speaking style – the style that matches their personality, character, and speech content, and the style that totally works for them.

I also learned that while it's great to be inspired by someone, it's even more important to know that what works for them will probably not work for you.

BE INSPIRED BY OTHERS, BUT COMMIT TO BEING YOU

Although I was upset by this event at the time, it was a valuable lesson for me to continue developing, practicing, and getting comfortable with my own speaking style.

This is the reason I want to emphasize to you how important it is to continue developing, practicing and getting comfortable with *your* own speaking style.

 Get comfortable with your speaking style through practice and trial and error. You may be inspired by another speakers' style, but it's important to be 100% authentically *you*.

I'm not saying that you shouldn't try new things or stretch yourself, because that's an important part of your growth as a speaker. However, when you are in front of your very important audience, stay true to the speaking style that matches your personality and your character, so that every time you speak, you are 100% authentically *you*.

The more you practice, the more you speak, and the more you get feedback from both individuals and technological means, the more easily you'll be able to figure out what feels most comfortable when you're in front of an audience.

And with that comfort level will come greater confidence, greater abilities, and greater impact.

HOW DO YOU KNOW WHAT WORKS – AND WHAT DOESN'T?

First, feedback is key. It can come from trusted friends, colleagues, and advisors – or perhaps a video recording that captures your speech, which you can review afterwards to see how your audience saw you. These resources are extremely helpful for you to understand what you *really* look like when you're presenting. And when you get information on what you look like to an audience, you can start making the adjustments that will make you look and feel more confident.

Start by recognizing what's good about your speaking style. Then take some time to objectively assess what you may need to work on to make it smoother and more authentic.

Maybe you pace too much. Maybe you fidget. Maybe you speak too quickly. Or maybe, like me, you speak with your hands so much that people suggest you tone down your "T-Rex arms." Once you understand what needs to be improved in your body language, you can be more conscious of it every time you speak so that the way you move does not distract your audience away from your message.

Ensuring that your body language, gestures, and movement are smooth and purposeful may take a little time, and it may take some trial and error. With enough practice, and continuous, conscious fixes and improvements, you'll get closer and closer to recognizing – and loving – your unique speaking style.

WHAT DO I DO WITH MY HANDS?

"What do I do with my hands while I'm giving a speech or a presentation?" is a very common question when it comes to body language. Generally, try to avoid the various hand movements described below.

- **Fidgeting.** It's usually within the first 30 seconds of any speech or presentation that we are most likely to fidget as we work to get comfortable in front of our audience. I have seen people put their hands in their pockets, take them out, put them back in, reach for papers, clue into the fact that they are fidgeting too much, and then try to stop and settle themselves. Be conscious of how much you are fidgeting, and have a backup plan in place if you discover that your nerves are taking over your hands.

- **Holding Anything Unnecessary in Your Hands.** The one exception to this rule is holding a wireless presenter (also known as a "clicker" to move your slides) or anything you need to pick up to show your audience. If you're holding a pen or paper, there's the possibility that you may start playing with it unconsciously. I've seen many speakers click their pens or fold their papers without even being conscious of it. Plus, if your hands are shaking due to nerves, it's made even more obvious when you're holding something. Fiddling around with papers has the added disadvantage of creating that "crinkling" noise, which is doubly distracting to your audience.

- **Place Your Notes on the Podium.** If you feel like you need to use your notes because you can't remember everything you want to say and are worried about blanking out, your best strategy is to put the notes down, but still within reach. Look at them when or if you need to, and then step away from them and return your attention to your audience when you regain confidence over your content.

- **Try Not to Distract Yourself – Or Your Audience – With What's on You.** That could mean playing with your rings, holding your hands too tightly, flipping or playing with your hair, scratching your arm, clasping your hands too tightly, or touching your glasses too often.

Here's what you *can* do with your hands instead.

- **Keep Them Above the Belt Line.** Speaking with your hands clasped below the belt can pull your posture into a slouching position, and can also give the impression of being less confident. When you are in front of a room, you want to project a position of leadership. So, keep your hands apart, elevated, open to the audience, and move them naturally.

- **Relax and Be Yourself.** It's OK to speak while your hands are moving, *and* it's OK to speak with your hands by your sides. You may find that you like to speak with your hands. It takes time to develop your speaking style, and it takes time to figure out what feels comfortable or not. As long as it fits your personality and your style, then go with it.

COORDINATING YOUR VOICE, BODY LANGUAGE, AND CONTENT

So far, this chapter has discussed how your body is constantly sending messages. Your audience will judge based on what they see *and* hear. As a result, you must make sure that *what* you say and *how* you say it are aligned.

Ask yourself, "Does my face, body and tone of voice match my content, and what I'm actually saying?"

Saying "I'm so happy to be here" with a frown on your face, or in a voice that is so low in volume that no one can hear you isn't convincing.

Saying "I think you'll really get excited when you hear about next quarter's strategy" in a shaky or monotone voice isn't convincing.

Saying "I hate to tell you this, but ..." with a smile on your face isn't convincing.

In all your presentations, be mindful that your content, gestures, and facial expressions match.

 *Not a* SUPER SPEAKER STORY

Distracting Movements – Distracted Audience

One of the students in the university public speaking class that I taught spent the first three minutes of a five-minute speech scratching her hand – continuously. Three entire minutes. After about a minute of watching this, the other students and I could see that she wasn't going to stop. We were probably all collectively wondering if she was going to scratch all her skin off (FYI: she didn't).

When she finished speaking, there was an awkward silence in the room. We couldn't give her feedback about the content of her message, because, well, who was even paying attention to what she was saying? We were all completely distracted by the hand scratching.

As it turns out, she had *no idea* that she was scratching her hand, or that she scratched it for such a long time. She didn't even feel the after-effects of three straight minutes of scratching. I couldn't believe her hand wasn't bleeding by that point.

Was she embarrassed when she found out? Yes, a little. But she was also extremely grateful to have learned of her potential for these distracting movements within the safety of our supportive class, and not in front of her employer, professors, or her peers in other classes.

Needless to say, I suspect that this is a mistake that she never, ever repeated.

 When giving a presentation, make sure that your content, gestures, and facial expressions are in line with each other.

Filter Out Filler Words

Let's address *how* you speak – the words of value and the words that distract, and the awkward silences that may not be awkward after all.

FILLER WORDS

For many of us, the use of words like "Uh," "Um," "Like," "You know," and "So" can easily get out of control if we're not conscious of them.

Filler words can ... um, like, you know ... become a distraction and break your connection with your audience.

These "filler" words aren't usually an issue when they're said a few times in a meeting or presentation. The problem is when they are used repetitively. That's when they become a distraction, because not only can they make the speaker look unsure of themselves, but they can also totally hurt the speaker's credibility.

Maybe these words find themselves into your presentations and conversations because you've been asked a tough question, you're nervous, or you haven't prepared and practiced enough. You may sometimes use them because you're feeling overly casual. Whatever the reason, while you don't have to focus on completely eliminating these words, you do have to make a valiant effort to control how often you say them.

Here are a few strategies to reduce using these words when on the stage, in front of the room, or even in an online meeting.

1. **Try to Hear – And Catch – Yourself Using Filler Words.** An important first step in ridding yourself of filler words is to become aware of when you use them. Record yourself, using audio or video, in a meeting or presentation and listen to all those cringe-worthy sounds – um, uh, like, you know, so, and whatever other iterations you may come up with. In addition, be on the lookout for their more sophisticated filler word cousins, such as "honestly," "ultimately," and "literally." You can't change what you're not aware of.

2. **Have Your Transitions Ready.** One of the reasons you may rely on filler words, especially the all-powerful "um," is to subtly tell the audience that you're not done talking yet. Instead of doing that, have some transitions ready, such as "Let's move on to talk about …" or "This brings me to my next point, which is …" or "As a recap to the previous point …" Having these go-to transitions ready will help you feel more natural, and more confident about your ability to leave behind the ums. (For other transition options, see pages 80–81.)

3. **Silence Instead of a Filler Word.** Silence can be powerful. In the past, I've had some clients ask me if it's preferable to say "um," rather than to have an awkward silence. My responses to this have varied between, "No" and "Define 'awkward silence.'" In other words, it is *not at all* preferable to say "um." There's more on the value of pausing in the next section.

As speakers, what we may perceive as an awkward silence, because we're desperately trying to find our words and get back on track, may be a false assumption. It's usually more likely that our audience perceives the silence as giving them an opportunity to reflect, because you're considering something important, or that you're taking your time to provide a good response.

Once you practice more often, get feedback from your trusted colleagues or friends, or video or audio record yourself, you'll become more aware of when and how these filler words show up in your presentations, what might trigger them, and how to consciously avoid using them.

You can't change what you're not aware of.

Your Filler Word Replacement Options

At your next presentation or communication, when you feel an "um" coming on, which you inevitably will, here's what you can try instead.

- Nothing.
- Stay silent.
- Let the pause linger.

Again, it's not necessary to eliminate all the filler words. They are a regular, natural form of casual conversation. We are simply looking to become more aware of when we use them, and minimize their occurrence whenever possible.

SPEAKING OF PAUSING

When you are speaking to an audience, you might consider too much silence as a sign of not being adequately prepared, extreme nerves, or just generally a bad presentation. You might want to avoid pausing because you believe that silence is awkward ... because you're naturally a fast talker ... or because you don't want the audience to think that you've forgotten what you want to say.

 **Pausing can be a powerful communication tool.**

As mentioned in the previous section, pausing is an important technique for speakers and can be beneficial to your presentation. In fact, even an unplanned pause can be perceived positively by the audience. But knowing where and when to put the pause is not always simple.

There are several strategic reasons why you would want to pause in your communications.

1. Grab attention
2. Add impact, drama, or anticipation
3. Give yourself time to think before you respond
4. Give your audience time to think about what you just said

5. Give your audience time to laugh

6. Transition to a new topic

7. Eliminate (or minimize) filler words

8. Take a sip of a drink

9. To breathe

The Best Spots to Pause

When you're creating your talk or outlining the main points that you want to cover, think about *where* in your speech you can pause most strategically. Where are you transitioning between ideas? Where do you want to build anticipation, allow a point or story the time to "land" on the audience, or create a greater impact? If you plan to move around or to pick up physical objects to show to the audience, a pause offers a subtle signal that something different is coming.

> *"The most precious things in*
> *speech are the pauses."*
>
> SIR RALPH RICHARDSON

And then – here's the important part – if you've decided in advance exactly where in your presentation you are going to pause, make sure that you provide yourself with some subtle cues to do it. A note in your script, your speaking notes, or your slides will help ensure that you don't get caught up in the moment and forget to take advantage of the opportunity to create a meaningful pause.

Silence could be your most powerful communication tool.

So … take a pause … and reflect on that!

SLOW DOWN WHEN YOU WANT TO SPEED UP

Sometimes you may start speeding up your rate of speaking due to nerves, excitement, because you're running out of time, or because you're ready to move towards the finish.

If you find that happening, stop. Once you start rushing through your content or slides, the audience may miss some important points of your presentation, and that's an easy way to disengage them.

The Podium – To Use It or Not to Use It

What is the best practice when it comes to using a podium? Should you use one if you have the option? Or is it always better to put yourself front and center of an audience to fully engage them?

Rest assured that you can still fully engage an audience when speaking from behind a podium. But (yes, there's always a "but"), it depends on *how* you use it. How you use the podium will be the difference between an unengaged audience and an audience that has just had a meaningful, valuable experience.

READING YOUR SPEECH FROM THE PODIUM

If you've ever sat through a presentation where the speaker stood at a podium reading their notes, you know that there's a huge potential for it to be a boring, frustratingly long experience for the audience.

But the fact is, depending on the room setup, when you are asked to speak at a meeting, conference, or other event, speaking at a podium might be your only option. And for situations when you may not have had time to prepare and practice adequately, you may choose to bring, use, and maybe even read from your speaking notes, from behind the podium.

Is reading your speech while standing at a podium an exercise in audience boredom and frustration? Not necessarily, as long as you follow a few important guidelines.

THE PROTECTION OF THE PODIUM

Let's be honest, a podium can be a very useful tool for a speaker. You can put your notes on it, it gives you something to hold onto, you get a little protection barrier from the audience (unless it's one of those clear plastic ones, in which case your audience can see *everything*).

Also, if you're behind a podium, you don't have to worry about the "rules" of body language or any other possibly distracting movements, because you won't be standing up in front of your audience. Right?

The answer to that would be a big "No."

There are a whole other range of distracting movements that a podium can tempt you to make, if you're not mindful of them.

Your hands may tap on the podium, you may hold onto it too tightly, you may lean back on your heels, or you may shift from one leg to the other. On top of that, reading your notes can lower your energy – thus affecting the energy of the entire room. There are three main reasons why this may happen.

Think you're safe because you'll be speaking from behind a podium? Think again!

1. Your focus is on your notes and, as a result, you're not making eye contact with the audience.

2. Reading your notes may result in you speaking in a more level, monotone voice.

3. You're already nervous enough standing up in front of your audience, so your voice won't be as loud and strong as it could be.

In short, you're disconnected from your audience.

HOW TO MAKE A PODIUM WORK FOR YOU

If you've got a presentation coming up where you know that you'll be standing at a podium and you need to read your notes, you've got to balance the need to present your content in a way that's comfortable for you with the need to keep your audience engaged, interested, and connected with you and your topic.

The great news is that this is entirely possible.

Here are eight essential tips to implement if you're going to speak from a podium and use – or even read – your notes, and still create a meaningful and engaging experience for your audience.

1. **Impact Words.** Go through your script and pull out the words that you want to emphasize for impact. If you practice in advance by reading your speech out loud several times – which you should certainly make the time to do before the big day – take note of which words or phrases require extra vocal impact. This has the dual benefit of helping you avoid speaking in a

boring monotone and making sure you vary your voice and keep it more conversational. In addition, it will highlight important points for the audience's benefit. Consider marking these impact words in **bold** or ALL CAPS, so that they're easy for you to see on your script.

2. **Know Exactly When You Need to Look Up at Your Audience.** Look at your audience when you say "you" or "we," when discussing a shared vision, telling a story, and during your Introduction and Conclusion, so that you have a better chance of connecting – and staying connected – with them. Consider circling these words in your script or creating another scripting cue that will remind you to look up from your script.

3. **Be Aware of Your Speaking Speed.** Don't speak too quickly. If people miss too many of your words, they'll stop listening to you altogether.

4. **Authenticity, Enunciation, Pausing … and Repeat.** If you're speaking quickly because you're excited, or because that's your speaking style, that's OK! However, you must still be mindful that your speaking speed may make it difficult for some members of your audience to follow. In this situation, try to enunciate your words, don't let them trail off at the end of sentences, and pause just before you make new points and between transitions. This adds impact to what you're saying and allows your audience the time to digest the important points.

5. **Voice Modulation and Inflection.** When you read your notes, it can be easier to fall into a monotone voice. Vary the speed, pitch, and volume at which you speak, so that you keep the speech more interesting to listen to. Your audience will respond better to your content if you present it in a more conversational tone, with more interest and excitement in your voice.

6. **Smile and Facial Expressions.** Are you happy to be there? Regardless of whether you are or aren't happy, you need to make sure that you look like you appreciate the opportunity to speak to the audience, and that you're grateful for the

attention that they're giving you. It really is a big privilege to be given that opportunity. At the same time, nerves, concentration, or deep focus can bring on "overly-serious face," which can affect how the audience connects with you. Try to be more aware of that, and "lighten up" where possible. It will make you look more approachable and friendly.

Overall, facial expression should match the emotional content. So what do you do if you're presenting a more serious topic? Start with a relaxed and neutral face. Make eye contact with your audience. Be authentic with the news that you're sharing so that you can stay connected with them throughout your presentation.

7. **Body Language DOs:** Stand straight, both feet on the ground in a parallel position. Keep both feet behind the podium. Watch your posture. And this bears repeating: Don't read your entire speech. Look up at your audience often, make eye contact throughout the whole room – not just those closest to or smiling at you.

8. **Body Language DON'Ts:** Do not bend your knee back and forth; lean on your hip, your elbow, or press back on your heel (so that the audience can see the bottom of your shoes); grasp the podium too tightly; tap your fingers on the podium; tap your foot on the ground; let your foot stick out the side of the podium; cross your legs; stretch your arms out over the podium to hold the farthest end of it; or hunch your shoulders.

What About Virtual Presentations?

We've all been called to deliver – and attend – virtual presentations, meetings, remote learning, and training. Managed well, a virtual presentation can be interactive, conversational, and fun. Managed badly, a virtual presentation can quickly bore, distract, and lose the attention of an audience.

As I've mentioned several times in this book, as speakers, it is our responsibility to make sure that the message that we are sending is received by our audience with maximum value. That means ensuring that the content is structured, engaging, and relevant, and that the delivery is smooth and seamless, regardless of whether we're speaking to them in person or via an online platform.

 Virtual presentations can be interactive, conversational, and engaging. Or they can be boring and energy-depleting. Your preparation can make the difference.

In a virtual environment, there are several common mistakes that can take away the audience's attention and make it more difficult to get your message across. Fortunately, many of these mistakes can be easily avoided.

Whether you're a speaker, facilitator, or raising your hand to ask a question or share a comment, here are eight easy fixes to make sure that you are showing up well, looking good, and maximizing your time in the virtual world.

1. **Make Sure that Your Camera Is at Eye Level.** Raise your laptop or your computer to get the camera at eye level. A standing desk or an adjustable laptop stand is useful, but you can just as easily use books or some boxes to get that extra lift. A tripod works well if you're connecting with your phone. Do whatever it takes so that no one has to look up your nostrils, stare at the ceiling, or have other random body parts in their immediate line of sight.

2. **Where Are Your Eyes Looking?** There are a lot of different places that you could look during a virtual presentation, but you need only look at the camera – or just slightly "off" camera. It can be tempting to look at yourself or at others on the screen when you're presenting, which is fine as long as you make sure that your audience perceives that you're making eye contact with them.

   Some people will give presentations looking at their laptop or at their second monitor. When this happens, they end up looking completely away from the screen and then only the side of their face is visible. It can be a challenge to connect with the speaker if you feel like they're not even looking at you, so be aware of your primary and secondary monitors, and through which one the audience can see you.

In the earlier days of virtual presentations, one trick that I used to remind myself to look directly at the camera was to draw arrows or messages like "look over here!" on a sticky note and put it right near my camera. It may sound silly, but it was effective, and it reminded me to keep my eyes where they were supposed to be.

3. **Fidgeting.** Body language is not just something that happens with in-person presentations. Watch out for fidgeting, swaying or rocking back and forth in your chair.

4. **Proper Lighting.** You don't necessarily need a professional lighting setup, but be mindful not to have your back to a window (it will make you look too dark to your audience), or other shadows or dark spots that can obscure people seeing you clearly. Good lighting will make you easier to watch, and even easier to listen to.

5. **Audio Quality – And Using the Mute Function.** Relying on your computer, tablet, or phone's microphone may not represent you – and your voice – as well as you'd like. Depending on your room setup, your audience may hear echoes or other distracting background sounds. Good audio is critical to making it easy for your audience to stay engaged with you. Headphones, ear buds, or external microphones can often be very useful – and not very expensive – investments to ensure that your voice is heard clearly and audibly.

6. **Your Background Setting – Too Busy, Cluttered, or Distracting?** While you are not necessarily expected to maintain a totally clean, distraction-free background throughout your online calls, meetings, or presentations, you do need to be aware that your background is probably being scrutinized by others in your call. Do your utmost to clean up as best you can. If working from home, clean up messy bookshelves, get rid of strange and unidentified background items, and please – no beds in the

background. If you choose to use virtual backgrounds, be careful that the ones that you choose aren't too over the top. Things like spaceships and beaches? Don't do it. And make sure that your body parts don't disappear into your virtual background or green screen whenever you move.

7. **Dress Well, Because It Still Matters.** Just as meetings still need agendas and structure, what you choose to wear on video calls still contributes to making a positive, or negative, impression. People getting caught wearing pajama pants (or no pants) on video calls are a definite no-no.

   Also, if you wouldn't wear a baseball hat to an in-person meeting, don't wear it to your virtual meeting. Dress for your video calls as if you were attending them in person.

8. **People Can Tell If You're Doing Something Else.** They can tell if you're checking your phone, working on something else, or otherwise not paying attention. Being a respectful meeting attendee is just as important as being a respectful speaker.

With virtual presentations, you can continue to get your message across in the most valuable, engaging way possible, and create an environment where your audience doesn't want to do anything else except listen to you.

The Opportunity to Impact Your Audience Is Limitless

If you've built a beautifully structured speech that is tailored for the specific needs, wants, and challenges of the audience, then you're on your way to a successful speaking experience.

*As a speaker, **how** you get your message across is as important as **what** you're saying.*

But if you fidget too much, your slides are too packed with information, your voice is too low, you speak too fast, you read your speech in a total monotone, you keep saying "um," or you're uncomfortable in your own skin, the best content in the world will not entice your audience to pay attention to what you're saying.

A presentation is about much more than getting up on stage, giving your speech, and getting it done. It's about making the most of your time in front of your audience for your personal and professional success, the success of your presentation, and the value that you can pass on to your audience. And speaking of time spent in front of your audience ... it's now time to turn our attention to the *actual* time spent in front of your audience – as your presentation day arrives.

CHAPTER 7

Stepping Up and Speaking Out: The "Big Day"

*"THERE ARE THREE SPEECHES
FOR EVERY SPEECH YOU MAKE –
THE ONE YOU PREPARED,
THE ONE YOU DID, THE ONE
YOU WISH YOU DID."*

Dale Carnegie

Here we are, our final chapter. To all you hardy souls who have made it to the end, may I say – you are amazing.

It's so exciting to have gone through this process with you, to create your engaging, structured, and compelling presentation that you can now use to share your message and expertise, position yourself as a leader, and get the results that you want.

So now, the final step to unleashing your ultimate speaking potential on your captivated audience is to get yourself ready for the final, exciting stages of preparation.

But before we turn our attention to that, let's take a minute to review everything that you now know about creating and delivering a powerful presentation.

- From Chapter 1, you learned about the problem with presentations, and how *you* are uniquely poised to fix that problem for the benefit of all your future audiences.

- From Chapter 2, you learned how to boost your confidence and manage your nerves, and how strong structure and audience connection will help you accomplish both.

- From Chapter 3, you learned how to get clear on your message and your audience *before* building your speech, to identify how to educate, inspire, and persuade them and create a meaningful experience, so that you could get the results you want.

Your next presentation is scheduled. Now what?

- From Chapter 4, you learned about the essential steps to build a structured presentation by using the Diamond – a tool that will forever change how you build your presentations.

- From Chapter 5, you learned about storytelling structure for both personal and professional stories, and how they bring immense value to a presentation by building an emotional connection with the audience and creating a more engaging, entertaining, and interesting speaking experience.

- From Chapter 6, you learned how to deliver your presentation smoothly, with focus, flow and finesse – both for in-person or virtual presentations.

So, what's left to talk about? It all comes down to the preparation and work on three major milestones.

1. *Before* the big day
2. *On* the big day
3. *After* the big day

Let's start with getting you ready to nail your next presentation!

Before the Big Day

Before the big day, here's what you can do to get yourself and your speech into fighting shape and control any nerves that may start bubbling up as presentation day gets closer.

While some of these tips were already addressed in Chapter 2, they are worth revisiting in the context of managing your nerves on the actual *day* of your presentation.

1. **Internalize Your Speech.** Internalizing your speech doesn't mean to memorize it, but to practice it – a lot, and out loud. Speech rehearsal is an incredibly important part of both managing your nerves and getting more comfortable with your content. You can do it on a treadmill, in the shower, while washing dishes, walking the dog, in front of a mirror, on the drive to work. And if it's a long presentation, and you can't find a large, uninterrupted chunk of time to rehearse, then breaking it up into smaller segments will still be very beneficial.

2. **Record It.** Use audio or video (or both), and then – here's the kicker – make the time to review it. Resist the urge to criticize yourself, and use this as an opportunity to improve your presentation. Review it from an outside perspective, as if you're objectively coaching a friend or colleague. Be kind to yourself, and recognize what you're doing well too.

3. **Test It Out in Front of a Live Audience.** Consider delivering your presentation in front of other people before landing on your final audience. It's a great way to get more comfortable with your content, and with yourself and your delivery style. Friends, family, colleagues, or even your pet might enjoy the show.

4. **What If You *Freeze*?** Have you ever gotten up in front of an audience and then forgotten *everything* you wanted to say the moment it was your turn to speak? "Brain freeze" can happen when you least expect it, so it's good to be prepared with a backup plan. Alleviate the worry of blanking out and forgetting what you want to say by bringing a one-page outline of your presentation with you. Leave it within reach and refer to it only if you need to. Just having this kind of outline close by can help you feel more secure.

5. **Make a List.** Create a list of everything that you'll need for the day of your presentation well in advance, so that there will be no last-minute searches. Extra batteries, backup copies of your

presentation, power and extension cords, computer dongles (if you need an Internet connection), an extra pair of shoes – anything and everything that you need for the day. Write it down, type it out – but don't leave it in your head.

6. **Shift Your Mindset.** Focus on the value that you can provide to the audience, instead of how nervous you feel.

 Record your presentation rehearsal, and make the time to review it. Recognize what you need to improve – but also take the time to acknowledge what you're doing right.

> *You don't have to be perfect. But you must be prepared, practiced, and professional.*

As we discussed in Chapter 2, after all this preparation, you may still feel nervous. That's OK. *Do the speech anyway.*

As you get closer and closer to presentation day, remember that your highest priority is to provide value to your audience. You do not have to deliver it perfectly. Being overly focused on perfect delivery is called "perfection paralysis," and it will waste your time and energy in ways that aren't at all productive. Release the pressure to be perfect and focus instead on sharing your message in the way that you prepared it.

On the Big Day

It's the day of your presentation. You've prepared all that you can, and you're ready to go. But the nerves are starting to creep up on you. Your heart is starting to beat too fast, the heat is rising in your face, and you can feel the butterflies starting the party in your stomach. On top of that, you want to remember your intro, nail those impact points, and look fully in control in front of the audience.

There's nothing to fear! Here are ten things to do when you want to be awesome on the day of your presentation.

1. SHOW UP EARLY

Get there at least an hour early. You don't want technical issues, surprise conversations, traffic, parking, or construction to wreak havoc on your carefully planned schedule. Organize all your equipment, handouts, your water bottle, your backup notes, so that everything you'll need is in the right spot. Check that the technology is working as it should. Check out your speaking area, get comfortable with it, and make sure that there are no obstructions or distractions, like wires on the floor, big posters behind you, big chairs, etc. Make it easy for your audience to see you from anywhere in the room. By the time they start to show up, the only thing that should be left for you to do is to greet them with a big smile.

For a virtual presentation, login at least a half-hour early to do all your tech checks: video, audio/microphone, lighting, background, screen sharing, polls, and anything else that you need to make sure that your presentation runs seamlessly.

2. BRING BACKUPS OF YOUR BACKUPS

We've talked about creating a backup plan in several different contexts throughout *From Nervous to Nailed It!*, because it is *the* inevitable truth in life that things don't always go exactly as planned.

Equipment can fail, batteries can run out, cords may be flayed, connections and plugs may not connect and plug as they should. Prepare yourself for what could go wrong. Extra batteries, HDMIs, uploading your presentation on alternate sources (i.e., Dropbox, Google Drive, Cloud-based backups, USBs), and sending a copy both to yourself and maybe even someone else attending the meeting (or the meeting planner) are useful contingency plans. Even with all that, things may still go wrong, but at least you'll have more reinforcement and will be ready to present despite the challenges.

3. BE READY WITH THE "OTHER" BACKUPS

Now it's time to talk about a true "wildcard" when it comes to giving presentations. Shoes!

The right shoes can help your posture; they can help your back, your knees, your ankles, and various other body parts; and they can make you look professional and fabulous.

Not Adapting for a Tech Failure

Several years ago, I attended a presentation where the speaker arrived early, got her computer and slides set up and was all ready to start on time ... and, then, just as she was about to start her presentation, her technology crashed. A total unexpected fail. The slides disconnected from the screen, and neither she, nor the tech support that came rushing in to help, knew why.

Her stress was palpable – and understandably so. While the IT team worked valiantly to resolve the issue, we all sat awkwardly and watched the struggle. After around 20 minutes, they got it up and running. As a result, she started her talk 20 minutes later than scheduled, and she further decided that she would finish 20 minutes later as well.

While it was a good presentation, going over time wasn't a great call. Many people had to leave before the presentation was finished, or right in the middle – in other words, right around the time that the presentation was originally scheduled to end – because it conflicted with what they had planned for the rest of their day. This was especially frustrating for those who specifically wanted to hear the speaker but had to miss part of her presentation because of the late start – and subsequent late ending time.

A better scenario? Give yourself five to ten minutes to try to fix the IT issue, and if it doesn't get fixed, then put a smile on your face, and be prepared to move ahead with your presentation without your slides. It's not your audience's fault if your technology doesn't work, and they shouldn't be inconvenienced because of it. Your slides are only a backup for the *real* star of the show (that would be you!), and you should know your content well enough to proceed without them.

The wrong shoes, however, can create a lot of discomfort and seriously affect how you're able to manage your day, and your ability to present.

If you know that you'll be standing on your feet in fabulously-stylish-but-not-meant-for-standing-all-day shoes, you may run into trouble if your feet start hurting. When I've got a full day of speaking, training, or networking in front of me, I'll start the day in my fancier shoes that are intended to make a good impression – otherwise known as the "super-stylin', high-heeled, toe-crushers" – and then switch to a second, more comfortable pair for when my feet can't function anymore.

 It's not easy to focus on your content and be your best self if your feet are hurting you. Choose professional shoes that you *know* are comfortable – and when in doubt, be prepared with some backup options.

If I'm speaking at a conference, which requires me to walk from the parking lot, and back and forth through a conference hall all day long, I will likely even bring a third pair of shoes – the flat, super-comfortable, not-at-all-stylish-but-at-least-my-feet-are-happy pair.

And this doesn't apply to women's shoes only! I've polled many of my male colleagues to better understand what kind of footwear issues they experience, and it turns out that many of them have suffered for style as well. Apparently, blisters, squeezed toes, and hard soles don't distinguish between men and women. The value of leather softeners, breaking them in around the house before taking them on their professional outing, and the biological barriers of expanding foot ligaments and tissues all came up in our discussions.

The overall conclusion? You don't have to sacrifice comfort for style. The most consistent recommendation shared was that whatever your gender, investing in high quality shoes will pay off in the long run. Spend the money on the right type of professional dress shoes and, not only will you impress people with your fancy footwear, but you will also be able to stay on your feet comfortably all day long.

What About Wardrobe Malfunctions?

Let's talk about your clothes. Choose clothing that looks professional, feels comfortable, and won't show sweat marks – because that can happen unexpectedly, and when it does, it's a distraction to everyone. Armpits sometimes have a mind of their own when you're wearing a button-down shirt or a blouse. You may want to invest in super-strong antiperspirant, or bring a backup sweater, blazer, or jacket if you need to cover up.

If you want to be really careful when it comes to your clothing, consider packing an extra outfit. This may help if you experience the sweat issue, or in case you spill anything on what you're wearing. And for women, if you're wearing nylons, do bring an extra pair, because we all know that they can tear simply by looking at them the wrong way.

4. GO TO THE WASHROOM – SERIOUSLY

We can get so caught up in the technology and room preparations that the important task of taking a trip to the washroom before your presentation can be forgotten. Do your business, and then check yourself top to bottom in the mirror. Make sure that everything is zipped and buttoned up; check your teeth; check your nose; and make sure that everything is tucked in properly. If you're wearing makeup, make sure that it isn't smudged and that you don't have lipstick on your teeth.

There's nothing worse than thinking that your audience can't take their eyes off you because of your magnificent presence and fascinating content, only to find out that what's mesmerizing your audience are pieces of spinach from your lunchtime salad that are stuck between your front teeth.

5. MEET YOUR ATTENDEES AT THE DOOR

Once you're back from the washroom and looking good from top to bottom, greet your audience as they walk through the door. If you're in a virtual meeting, greet them as they arrive to the platform. This allows you to make a connection with a few audience members and "warm up" the room.

6. SAY "YES!" TO THE MICROPHONE

If you're going to be speaking in a large room and you are offered a microphone, take it. If there is any doubt that people may not be able to hear you, take it. If you feel uncomfortable with a microphone and are sure that you can speak loudly enough throughout the presentation, you are wrong, so take it. Your audience should never have to struggle to hear your presentation. If they do, there's a strong likelihood that they'll simply "check out" and stop paying attention – and you will have to work extra hard to get that attention back.

7. HAVE WATER NEARBY

If you're feeling nervous, if you speak for a long time, or if you haven't drunk enough throughout the day, speaking can suck the moisture right out of you (which, as you remember from Chapter 2 can also happen as part of the fight-or-flight response). Luckily, all you need to do is have some water nearby and take a sip when necessary. Some good times to take a sip may be in your speech transitions, if someone is asking you a question, if you ask a question to your audience and are waiting for the answer, or if you're showing a video in your presentation. If you're using a glass, keep it within reach, but far enough away from your computer in case of accidental spills.

When delivering virtual presentations, consider keeping a water bottle nearby (with a tight-fitting lid), or a short, wide glass that is far less likely to get accidentally knocked over if you get overly excited with your hand gestures when speaking.

8. WATCH YOUR TIME

It can be hard to keep track of time when you're speaking. Boardrooms, conference rooms, or your home office don't always have a clock on the wall, which means that *you* are fully responsible for knowing your start and end times. In the past, I used a small travel alarm clock set up right in front of my computer, which is discreet and effective. Other times, I've set my wristwatch on the table right next to my computer, or on the podium, or wherever there's a flat surface.

The key word here is "discreet." If you use your smartphone to watch your time, just be mindful that the very action of looking at your phone during a meeting or presentation can be perceived as unprofessional. However, leaving it on a desk and glancing over at the time when you need to can be done in a very subtle way.

I once sat through a presentation with a speaker who was so concerned with the time that he checked his watch at least every two to three minutes – complete with a great flourish of the wrist. It left me with a lasting lesson of how easy it was to distract an audience with what he must have thought was just a simple flick of the wrist.

Doing a subtle timing check is much easier when in a virtual meeting or giving an online presentation. You can set a timer, use a watch, a smartphone, your computer's clock, or whatever is most useful for you.

9. "POWER POSING" YOUR WAY TO CONFIDENCE

In her famous TED talk,[15] Amy Cuddy shows how "power posing" – standing in a posture of confidence, even when we don't feel confident – can affect testosterone and cortisol levels in the brain, and might have an impact on our chances for feeling stronger and more confident, thereby leading to greater success in our lives. In essence, when you pretend to be powerful, you are more likely to feel powerful.

*According to a well-known TED talk, when you pretend to be powerful, you are more likely to **feel** powerful.*

I have actually put power posing to the test. Several years ago, right before getting on stage at a large conference where I felt particularly nervous, I thought it might help relieve my anxiety. I locked myself in a bathroom stall, put my hands on my hips, stood up tall, and waited for that powerful feeling to take over.

Did it work?

Well, yes and no. The truth is, I felt a bit silly going through this routine in a bathroom stall. I may have even had a little laugh about it (internally, of course). What I did learn, however, is that because I felt a bit silly and laughed at myself, I momentarily disconnected from my feelings of nervousness, which helped relieve some stress and made me feel better.

Maybe I didn't feel truly powerful in that moment, but it did help me get into a more positive mindset, which is exactly what I needed at the time.

What if you try power posing, and you *still* feel nervous? That's OK. Let it go. Ultimately, the audience doesn't really care how you feel. What they want is to get valuable content from your presentation.

10. HAVE FAITH IN YOURSELF!

If you've prepared, practiced, and done everything on this list, have faith that everything will be as it should be. Your presentation doesn't have to be perfect. It just has to be relevant for your audience's needs.

After your speech, take note of what worked well and what didn't. Adjust, tweak, and change your methods for your next presentation until you develop a system and style that works best for you.

The day of your presentation can be full of surprises. Just know that you've got this! If you've done the work, rest assured that your speaking awesomeness will be evident for all to see.

A "BIG DAY" NEAR-CATASTROPHE: HOW MY AWESOME SHOES NEARLY RUINED MY PRESENTATION

Years ago, I was hired to give a full-day training program to a group of 25 executives on how to master their public speaking skills. So I started to plan for it by going through all my training checklists. I targeted my materials to the group. I planned out each and every moment, piece of content, and individual or group exercise for the day. And then, closer to the day, I considered another important detail – my shoes.

I ended up with a conservative-yet-moderately-stylish-but-still-professional pair of black Mary Jane shoes. Thick, stable 2.5-inch heels. Comfortable enough to allow me to stand for the greater part of an eight-hour day.

Or at least that's what I thought.

Fast forward to the day of the training. At 9:00AM, we started with a bang. Solid content, engaged audience, the connection was being actively established.

Excellent.

At 9:45AM, we were moving right along, well into the first part of the morning, and everything was going exactly as planned. But wait, what was that unpleasant prickly sensation creeping into my feet?

It was pain, my friends. It felt like thorny, cactus-like needles poking into every inch of the bottom of my foot.

Turned out that my conservative-yet-moderately-stylish-but-still-professional pair of black Mary Jane shoes with the thick and stable

2.5-inch heels that were supposed to allow me to stand for the greater part of the day had failed me miserably.

At 10:30, we reached our first break. At this point, I practically crawled to the washroom, my feet throbbing with pain. I hauled myself up onto the counter right next to the sink, so that I could have a few minutes off my feet.

Yes, in full professional attire, I went to the washroom and *sat* on the counter next to the sink.

I took off my shoes – fully knowing that taking my shoes off while they're in pain (and probably swelling) was probably the last thing that I should be doing, as there was a risk that I wouldn't be able to get them back on afterwards. But the prospect of keeping them *on* my feet was even worse.

And then I prayed for a miracle, so that I could stand up not only for the rest of the day, but even just for the next ten minutes.

At this point, the only thing that was going through my mind was, "Why are these shoes so awful?!?" That was quickly followed by, "My feet are killing me and I didn't bring another pair of shoes and now I have to put my shoes back on and stand in front of this audience in a very professional way while pretending that little needles aren't sticking into my feet and blisters aren't forming and what the heck am I going to do and is it time to go home yet?!?"

Not necessarily the mindset you need if you really want to ace the day.

Especially not when you're shifting from foot-to-foot to alleviate the pain, while simultaneously instructing the audience on the importance of not shifting from foot-to-foot while giving presentations because of how distracting it can be.

Ultimately, I made it through the day. I adjusted part of the morning to make the training elements more conversational, which gave me the opportunity to sit down. At lunch, I sat down. In the afternoon, the participants went through some individual and group exercises, which gave me a chance to, you guessed it, sit down.

As the day went on, it seemed that no one was able to sense the searing pain coming out of my excruciating shoes except for me.

Thank goodness for small miracles.

When the day was mercifully over, my feet were so numb with pain that I could barely feel them anymore, which, in retrospect, may have been a good thing by that point.

My obvious learning from that day was that I had to make a better footwear plan for my future training sessions. These once-reliable, go-to, training-day shoes had to be fired – and then replaced with a more reliable, yet professional and stylish, pair.

What I knew for sure was that the experience of sitting on a washroom countertop and praying for an end to the prickly pain in my feet was not ever going to be repeated.

Preventing Future Shoe-Related Catastrophes

As mentioned earlier in this chapter, both women and men can suffer from the pain of wearing sub-optimal shoes. In doing a little more research on how to prevent foot pain, I learned that physiologically, standing is like walking. Both activities increase energy, burn extra calories, tone muscles, improve posture, increase blood flow, and ramp up metabolism.[16]

If standing and walking can do all that, we most certainly need to be kind to our feet.

Standing is like walking. It increases energy, burns extra calories, tones muscles, improves posture, increases blood flow and ramps up metabolism. So it's important to take care of our feet by wearing the right shoes!

Five Ways to Care for Your Fabulous Feet

When we stand up to give presentations, spend long hours on our feet or have to walk long distances, there are a few guidelines that we can use to prevent or manage foot pain, and take care of our overall long-term foot health.

1. Make sure you wear your size. This may seem obvious, but apparently lots of women squeeze into shoes that are a size smaller, which is a big no-no. Men don't always end up in the proper size shoe either, so being mindful of getting the right size, including the right width, is important to avoid problems.

2. If you choose to wear heels, supportive straps up to your ankle and/or a covered shoe with a peep toe for high heels can help prevent some pain problems. The more support your foot has, the more comfortable it is. This means that slip-on high heels are not always a good idea, because they have a higher likelihood of causing pain due to lack of foot support.

3. Feet will swell after hours of standing, especially if you're wearing heels. Therefore, if you take them off when they start hurting, it will be even harder – and more painful – to put them back on.

4. Get gel or foam inserts to put in your shoes to give added comfort to the bottom of your feet.

5. If you've done all that you can and your feet are still suffering, it might be time to consider arch supports or orthotics for additional foot care, safety, and comfort, or be willing to invest more money in a higher quality or specialty shoe.

Given how much our feet support us in our day-to-day lives, we need to make sure that we support them as well.

A Plan in Progress

I gave another full-day training program several weeks after my sit-on-the-bathroom-counter incident and tried a different tactic. Flat, comfy shoes on the way to the client, during the set-up, at lunch, and at the end of the day. Another pair of conservative-and-moderately-stylish-but-still-professional heels during the training, complete with supportive straps and gel inserts.

How did it go, you may ask?

I wish I could say that my feet were bathed in a soft glow of warmth and comfort, as if I was walking on a cloud, for the full eight-hour day.

They were not.

To be fair, I got a solid three hours of comfort out of these babies before the pain needles started to creep in. But by that point, we had reached lunch. I planned some group work in the afternoon, which afforded me a little more sitting time.

Thankfully, it was not nearly as bad as what I had experienced a few weeks earlier. There was no shifting from side-to-side, no throbbing pain, and, best of all, there was no sitting on random washroom countertops.

By the time we got to lunch, I did relent on my footwear rules, and changed into my backup shoes – flat, no heel, and, dare I say, oh-so-comfortable. By that point, first impressions were done, and any opinions that my audience had about me – and my dazzling footwear – were already set. I very gratefully put on the flat shoes that I had so condescendingly shunned earlier.

Funnily enough, about a month after that training session, I attended a conference where the speaker was a fairly well-known TV personality, author, entrepreneur, mother-of-four-kids, and millionaire. When she got on stage, she was wearing a spectacularly high (and very lovely!) pair of what must have been 4- or 5-inch heels, which were easily viewable because the stage was at eye-level and on full display. As she started her presentation, one of the first things I thought was, "Those shoes are truly fabulous! But how on earth will she stand in them for an entire hour?"

Within five minutes of starting her speech, she paused, looked at the audience, and said, "I hope you guys don't mind, but I have to take these shoes off. I just got off a plane, they're already swollen, they're so high, and they're killing my feet. I can't have a proper chat with you unless I take them off."

And she did the rest of her one-hour presentation in bare feet.

No backup shoes. Not even backup socks.

I'm not a celebrity, so I don't think that I can't get away with speaking to an audience in bare feet. However, I now bring two (and sometimes three) pairs of shoes to every speaking engagement, to hedge my bets and increase my options to keep the pain at bay.

You simply can't present effectively if your feet are killing you.

After the Big Day

You did it! Congratulations!

FIRST, CELEBRATE!

Before anything else – however you feel you may have done in your presentation, what went right and what went wrong, what you messed up and what you nailed – first and foremost, take the time to recognize your accomplishment. Acknowledge what you did well. Give yourself credit. It may not have gone *exactly* according to plan, but your audience didn't necessarily know your plan. And what you gave them may have been exactly what they needed to know at that time.

 **What's the very first thing you need to do after giving your presentation? Recognize your accomplishment!**

Also, take a moment to recognize that there are many people in the audience who may be too afraid to give a presentation, and simply too nervous to do what you just did.

You may not even know who may have been inspired by you, your content, your delivery style, your confidence (whether you felt confident or not), and your overall presentation, and, as a result, resolved to make a change in their lives – or resolved to step up in front of an audience and share *their* expertise at a future date.

But what if you forgot a whole section of your speech? Or you were stumped by a question you received? What if you went off on a tangent and couldn't easily find your way back, or felt convinced that your audience could tell how nervous you were? Is it possible that someone in the audience yawned and threw you off your game, that you said "um" a few times more than you wanted to, or that you thought of the perfect story only *after* the presentation ended?

Some of that may have happened. All of that may have happened. But that's OK! As *From Nervous to Nailed It!* has demonstrated repeatedly, you don't have to be perfect. You have to be prepared, share a meaningful message, and deliver value. And if that's what you did, even in an imperfect way, then congratulations! You delivered a presentation successfully!

HOW DO YOU KNOW IF YOUR SPEECH WAS ACTUALLY *GOOD*?

What happens if you've devoted time and effort building a presentation, and, then, after delivering it, generally had *no idea* whether the audience loved it, liked it, didn't like it, or just barely tolerated it?

Early in my speaking career, I had the opportunity to speak at a leadership conference targeted to women who worked in the automotive industry. I had interviewed several of the attendees in advance, so that I could craft a presentation tailored specifically to them, with a focused message, structured content, a strong opening and closing, engaging stories that were relevant to their industry, crystal-clear points, and smooth transitions. I acted out my stories, practiced extensively, made edits. I audio recorded myself, listened to it, made more edits, sent it to colleagues for feedback, made more edits, and practiced again. I went step-by-meticulous-step through the Diamond to create something that was structured, engaging, impactful, and *just right* for this audience.

I was confident that I had crafted a strong speech that would land perfectly on a smiling, interested, and laughing-at-the-appropriate-moments audience.

The day of the speech came.

While I was on stage, I worked it. My energy was high, I remembered the stories, got the transitions right, and even when I didn't fully stick to the script, the content was so deeply ingrained that I said what had to be said at all the right spots.

Phew! An hour later, I was done.

But I had no idea if they liked it.

You see, through all my practice, edits, visualizations, and more practice, I envisioned the audience sitting up high in their seats, leaning forward, laughing loudly, smiling and nodding through the entire speech.

But here's what really happened. Yes, some people smiled and nodded, some laughed at the right spots (but not all), some took notes, some just sat back in their chairs and listened, with what seemed like a blank expression on their faces.

After all that work, time, and effort I put into creating my speech, I had no idea if my presentation hit the mark or missed it altogether.

Many of my clients share similar stories. "When I give a presentation at work, even if I've worked hard on it and I know it's got the right information, the people I'm presenting to look at me with blank faces. How am I supposed to know what they're thinking? How do I know if the presentation was a success, or if they even liked me and what I said?"

At the heart of this issue is confidence – not a confidence in public speaking or a lack of nerves when getting in front of your audience, but rather, a confidence that what you have prepared, researched, understood, practiced, revised, and worked hard on will result in a presentation that is relevant to your audience.

 **Having trouble "reading" the audience? Wondering if their blank faces or crossed arms mean that they're disengaged? It's far more likely that these blank faces represent people who are focusing on your message and what they're learning from you.**

When you can honestly say that you've done that, then you can be fairly confident that your message was received well, even if their faces don't always show it.

Those blank faces in the audience can be intimidating. What I've learned, however, is that blank faces do not necessarily mean that an audience is bored or unengaged. Yes, it's possible that instead of focusing on your presentation, some people may be thinking about what they'll have for dinner, a past conversation with a friend, or when they'll be able to pick up their dry cleaning. But it's far more likely that these blank faces reflect people who are focusing on your message, people who are making connections regarding how they can integrate what they're learning from you into their professional or personal lives, and people who are considering how differently they could have handled a past situation if they had previously learned the information that you're presenting.

When my presentation was done, I sought out the event planner immediately to get her feedback. "Did the content meet your objectives?" (I thought this was way less needy than saying, "So, did you like it?") The event planner told me that she noticed everyone listening very attentively and taking copious notes, and that, in fact, she was extremely happy with how it turned out.

For all the time that I spent doubting myself, I could have just been … *not* doubting myself.

I stayed on at the event, and over the rest of the day had a chance to speak with many other women who stopped to talk about their public speaking challenges and revealed how some of the stories that I shared really resonated with them. Many of those "blank" faces I saw while I was speaking were actually very friendly, animated, and receptive when we were casually talking. In fact, many of those "blank" faces were simply focusing on what I was saying and determining how to apply these new ideas to their lives.

That day, I learned that just because we don't get the reaction that we expect doesn't mean that our message isn't having the desired effect.

Just because we don't get the reaction that we expect doesn't mean that our message isn't having the desired effect.

The next time that you give a presentation and are having trouble "reading" the audience reaction, you can be confident that if you've spent the time, done the research, put your full focus and expertise into it, and crafted something that is structured, engaging, and relevant to your audience, your message will be received in the right way.

And have confidence that behind those blank faces, there are some people who are *loving* your message – and loving *you*.

REVIEW, EVALUATE, AND PLAN FOR THE NEXT ONE

Now that you have delivered your presentation, what do you do next?

Get Feedback

Get feedback from those who understand what you want to achieve and can give you an unbiased opinion of your presentation. Get feedback from trusted advisors, supervisors, colleagues, and friends. And if you really want to take your skills to the next level, consider investing in a coach who can help you get where you want to be.

But be aware that not all feedback is created equally. I once had a client who got feedback from her coach that focused on how her eyebrows moved too much, her voice was too nasally, and her nose was too upturned. If you get feedback like this – please, please ignore it. The mark of good feedback is someone who offers insights based on who you are and where your natural talents lie. They should be able to help you refine your speaking skills so that you can speak in a way that is more impactful, engaging, and confident, and in a way that is natural and authentic to you. If they start picking on your face, your body, or other parts that are authentically *you* – leave them behind!

What if You Get Negative Feedback?

Picture this scenario. You give a presentation to an audience of 50 people. In the evaluations or conversations afterwards, you find out that 48 of these individuals rated your presentation very positively.

The remaining two individuals didn't react as positively. They didn't like your message. They didn't like your slides. They didn't like your hair. They share criticisms that make you doubt all the positive feedback and second-guess your content – and yourself.

But let's recap. Forty-eight people had a very positive experience; two people didn't.

So despite the fact that the majority of our audience rated the presentation highly, what very irrational thing do we *still* do?

We focus on the criticism, of course!

But here's what we should do instead.

Take All Feedback Seriously, Except ...

When it comes to feedback, a good rule of thumb is to take *all* feedback seriously. However, we must still remember that negative comments are generally based on personal taste and subjective opinions. Don't be too quick to change your presentation unless you hear the same comment either from a significant number of audience members or across multiple presentations.

It can be surprisingly easy to allow one or two negative comments to outweigh the positive ones. Go easy on yourself, don't take it personally, and accept that it's one person's opinion.

That said, sometimes this kind of feedback can be very valuable to help strengthen your message, or to learn of certain delivery distractions that you didn't know you were exhibiting.

You need to be able to put your ego aside and objectively assess if the feedback is valuable in making your message even stronger. Ultimately, *you* get the final decision as to whether you will use the feedback as a tool to help you keep improving, or discard it if it doesn't feel right for you.

What Do You Do with All This Feedback?

Dedicate yourself to consistent improvement. Assess what went well, and what could have been better. What worked? What didn't? Recognize it all, and dedicate yourself to making it better, learning from your mistakes, and constantly striving to improve your presentations.

And most importantly – keep speaking! Whether you're shy or confident, an experienced speaker or just starting out, keep speaking. Some people in your audience *really* need to hear your message. The results you want will come from being authentic, and sharing your expertise in a structured, focused, and engaging way.

Keep adjusting, tweaking, and changing your methods for your next presentation until you develop the system that works best for you. And then you can rock it every time!

FINAL WORDS

"THE ONE EASY WAY TO BECOME WORTH 50 PERCENT
MORE THAN YOU ARE NOW – AT LEAST – IS TO HONE YOUR
COMMUNICATION SKILLS – BOTH WRITTEN AND VERBAL."
Warren Buffett

The Key to Success

The ability to communicate in a clear and engaging way is no longer a "soft" skill. It's your key to success in almost any field. It's in high demand … and it never goes out of style.

In order to communicate, collaborate, and connect with your team, your colleagues or your audience, you must be able to narrow a presentation down to the essentials, communicate your vision in a meaningful way, and create a valuable experience for both you and your audience.

With Great Power Comes Great Responsibility

As a fan of superhero comics, movies, and trivia, I find that one of the most well-known phrases, known by even non-superhero fans, is credited to Peter Parker's (aka Spiderman) Uncle Ben, who gives him the wise advice, "With great power, comes great responsibility." Use your powers wisely, Spiderman – and use them in the right circumstances.

As we have so often heard, knowledge is power. If you are lucky enough to have unique knowledge, skills, and talent – your own unique superpowers – then *you* have a responsibility to use them wisely.

I used to teach a public speaking course for graduate students – students pursuing a Master's degree, Ph.D., or postdoc in every field from law to sociology, bioresource chemical engineering to political science, dentistry to art history, and everything in between. Many of these students registered for the class to get over a fear of public speaking, but also because they knew that there would be many presentations in their future and wanted to be proactive about improving their speaking skills.

At the start of every semester, I would meet a new group of students. One of the first things I did was to thank them. I thanked them because I truly appreciated how individuals at that level of education, who had done so much schooling, so much research, and had such a deep expertise in a particular subject, would be taking this step to help them share it with the world, and not let a fear of public speaking hold them back.

The fact is, you don't need a master's degree or Ph.D. to have a message that shares knowledge, changes lives, and makes an impact on this world. It's not in anyone's interest for you to keep your expertise, education, and experience hidden, and to hold back the light that you can shine on other people's lives, because of a general discomfort or fear of public speaking.

Making Your Way to the Top

Now that we're near the end of this book, it seems fitting to share one of my very favorite speaking-related quotes that has always deeply resonated with me.[17]

> Those who learn how to stand up and speak in front of a group of people and don't have a fear of public speaking are automatically leaders. If you can overcome your fear of speaking, you move into the top 20% of the world. If you can actually learn to speak in a way that makes a difference in somebody's life, you become part of the top 20% of the 20% of the world.

When you made the decision to invest your time and energy into *From Nervous to Nailed It!*, I suspect that your motivation may have been to improve your presentation skills, so that you could share your expertise, speak with confidence, and position yourself as a leader.

If you have followed the tips, techniques, and insights provided in all the previous chapters and have applied them to your presentations in a way that creates value, relevance, and impact for your audience, I think it's safe to say that you have now securely moved into the top 20% of the 20%.

And for that I say, "Well done!"

Your Next Important Steps

You may wonder how, after all your hard work and great results, you can continually remain in the top 20% of the 20% on a long-term basis. There's an easy answer to that.

Keep speaking!

Do the work. Create your high-impact presentation, then create another, and keep speaking up and getting in front of audiences to share your expertise, experience, and message. Get feedback from trusted sources. Edit. Improve. Take chances. Push yourself.

Finesse it, practice it, and then get out in front of an audience and deliver it!

Not only will you be building your credibility, authority, and visibility, but you may also be inspiring others – inspiring them towards change, and inspiring them to push themselves to speak up, deliver more presentations, and present with confidence. Essentially, you may be motivating them to *be more like you.*

With the strategies laid out in this book, you can now step out in front of an audience – whether it's an audience of 1, 100 or 1000 – and get your point across with passion, persuasion, and power.

You now have the tools to get the new client, the job, the promotion, or the recognition that you want and deserve.

You now have processes that allow you to experience speaking success over and over again.

You are now in a position not only to educate audiences with your message, but to inspire them, and persuade them to action. You will be seen as a trusted leader, and as someone who creates change, speaks with impact, and provides value to others.

I can't wait to see you out there.

Your audience is waiting …

END NOTES

Chapter 2: The Little Speaker Who Couldn't: Confidence

[1]John Montopoli, "Public Speaking Anxiety and Fear of Brain Freezes" (February 20, 2017): https://nationalsocialanxietycenter.com/2017/02/20/public-speaking-and-fear-of-brain-freezes/.

[2]First described and labeled in the 1920s by physiologist Walter Cannon. See also two Ted Talks on the subject: https://www.ted.com/talks/mikael_cho_the_science_of_stage_fright_and_how_to_overcome_it and https://www.ted.com/talks/joe_kowan_how_i_beat_stage_fright

[3]Albert Mehrabian, *Silent Messages: Implicit Communication of Emotions and Attitudes* (Belmont, CA: Wadsworth Publishing Company, Inc., 1971).

Chapter 4: Your Secret Weapon for All Your Presentations: Structure

[4]Nancy Duarte, *Resonate: Present Visual Stories that Transform Audiences* (John Wiley and Sons, 2010).

[5]Nancy Duarte, *Resonate*, at pages 100-101.

[6]Hermann Ebbinghaus, *Memory: A Contribution to Experimental Psychology* (New York City: Teachers College, Columbia University, 1913).

[7]Ray Ehrensberger, "An experimental study of the relative effectiveness of certain forms of emphasis in public speaking. *Speech Monographs* (1945) 12, 94–111. doi: 10.1080/03637754509390108.

Chapter 5: Seriously Skilled Storytelling: The Shine

[8]See: https://blog.hubspot.com/marketing/storytelling

Chapter 6: Putting It All Together: Let's Do This!

[9]See: https://www.forbes.com/sites/nickmorgan/2011/03/30/why-we-fear-public-speaking-and-how-to-overcome-it/#2154fa7c460b

[10]Molly St. Louis, "How to Spot Visual, Auditory, and Kinesthetic-Learning Executives: If Your Great Ideas Are Being Overlooked, Perhaps It's Time to Communicate Them Differently" Inc.com (Aug 1, 2017): https://www.

inc.com/molly-reynolds/how-to-spot-visual-auditory-and-kinesthetic-learni.html.

11 See: https://www.inc.com/molly-reynolds/how-to-spot-visual-auditory-and-kinesthetic-learni.html

12 See: https://www.smashingmagazine.com/2018/11/inclusive-design-accessible-presentations/

13 See: https://www.colourblindawareness.org/colour-blindness/

14 All these speakers can be viewed via a search on TED.com, except for Steve Jobs.

Chapter 7: Stepping Up and Speaking Out: The "Big Day"

15 See: https://www.ted.com/talks/amy_cuddy_your_body_language_may_shape_who_you_are

16 See: JustStand.org

Final Words

17 Dr. John Demartini is a human behavior expert, author, and speaker.

ACKNOWLEDGEMENTS

It takes a village to write a book. And *From Nervous to Nailed It!* was truly a labor of love that took a long, long time to come to fruition.

What fueled my passion were the people I met along the way who conquered their fear of speaking up, and then found confident, well-spoken and incredibly capable powerhouses lying within, waiting to spring forth. So much gratitude for them.

There are some other very important people I would like to thank who made this book possible. I have learned from and been supported by so many wonderful individuals over the years, and they deserve a tremendous amount of credit. I apologize in advance for those I may have missed.

My mastermind colleagues and early readers for their time, generosity, and invaluable advice in reviewing the book in the early stages, while also providing excellent advice in the title and design phases. Thank you Glynis E. Devine, Lisa Mendelovici, Paul Frazer, PhD, Nanci Murdock, Ruth Nix, Ravi Tangri, Chris Bauer, PhD, and Michael Kerr. I could not have done this without you.

To my Focus Five friends who helped me birth the Diamond in one magical, fortuitous day. Sarena Miller, Liliana De Leo, Dahna Weber, Tina Romano, and Carrie Katz, thank you for listening to me describe my vision of what I was trying to accomplish and for helping me translate it into a framework that changed everything about my business. Thanks also for the sisterhood, the great conversations, and the delicious snacks.

The conventions and workshops I attended with my dear colleagues and friends at the Canadian Association of Professional Speakers from the past decade were always game-changers. I would like to name every single brilliant, generous, and innovative soul in this association who provided both loving support and the occasional kick-in-the-pants when needed, but that would require a whole other book. So for now, I would like to give special acknowledgment to Nabil Doss, whose encouragement, advice, and friendship have been such an important part of my CAPS journey, Les Kletke who generously shared his expertise as a book coach, and Toni Newman, who helped me craft the concept of the Killer Presentation Model around her dining room table.

To my coaching and training clients, who inspire me every day. Thank you for the great work that you do in this world, and for showing others the level of success that is possible.

To clients, colleagues, friends, and family who were on the receiving end of my many e-mails for questions relating to titles, design, colors, endorsements, and exactly how long the section on shoes should be, thank you for being so patient with me and sharing your insights to help me make these decisions. And thank you to the amazing mentors, friends, clients, and colleagues who wrote the endorsements that you saw in the front of this book.

Huge gratitude goes to Catherine Leek, my extremely talented editor who offered suggestions, support, editorial guidance and encouragement throughout this entire project, which lasted quite a bit longer than she bargained for. I suspect it's because I enjoyed her collaboration so much and just didn't want to let her go. Her kindness, friendly e-mails, and constant understanding of my missed deadlines were very appreciated. Many thanks also to my book designer Kim Monteforte, who understood exactly what I wanted this book to look like, and made it happen.

A very special mention goes to my mom, Lena Baum. Growing up, when I would get upset and want to address the person with whom I was displeased, she would usually encourage me to stay quiet, "turn the other cheek," and not talk back. But at other times when I *did* speak up and step outside of my comfort zone, she would secretly give me a proud "side-eye" and a happily-muttered "good for you!" I know that she was with me while I was writing this book, and I believe she would have thought that it was pretty cool.

And finally, to Mike and Alex. Thank you for your support and encouragement, for putting up with me in my semi-frazzled state throughout this process, and for sharing my excitement at getting this book finished.

ABOUT THE AUTHOR

Suzannah Baum is a presentation and leadership communication strategist, executive speech coach, and speaker. She works with organizations and business professionals who want to position themselves as leaders by communicating with more confidence, impact, and connection.

Through in-person or virtual training programs, workshops, executive speech coaching, online learning, and keynotes, Suzannah shares essential presentation and business communication strategies and techniques that can be used to turn every speaking opportunity into a rewarding and results-driven experience.

Suzannah's ideas on building better presentations and enhancing confidence have been featured in the Huffington Post, Global TV News, Breakfast TV Montreal, CJAD radio, and Elle Canada. She holds certifications in the DISC™ Model of Human Behavior and as an eSpeakers Virtual Presenter, and has served on the National Board of the Canadian Association of Professional Speakers (CAPS), as well as being a past Chapter President.

Suzannah is forever on the lookout for a pair of beautiful, high-heeled shoes that she can wear for more than four minutes, absolutely loves to hear the stories of how her clients nail their presentations, and always travels with chocolate.

Suzannah lives in Montreal, Canada, with her husband, son, and budgie.

WORK WITH SUZANNAH

Ready to unleash your ultimate speaking potential?

To book Suzannah for a training program,
coaching or event, please call
+1(514)247-1761
or email at
suzannah@suzannahbaum.com

suzannahbaum.com

linkedin.com/in/suzannahbaum

facebook.com/suzannahbaumpublicspeaking

twitter.com/suzannahbaum

instagram.com/suzannahbaum

youtube.com/suzannahbaum

Manufactured by Amazon.ca
Bolton, ON

33146809R00114